W9-ACE-900

GLOBALVIEWPOINTS

Climate Change and Population Displacement

Other Books in the Global Viewpoints Series

GLOBALVIEWPOINTS

Climate Change and Population Displacement

Marcia Amidon Lusted, Book Editor

GREENHAVEN
PUBLISHING

Published in 2020 by Greenhaven Publishing, LLC
353 3rd Avenue, Suite 255, New York, NY 10010

Copyright © 2020 by Greenhaven Publishing, LLC

First Edition

All rights reserved. No part of this book may be reproduced in any form
without permission in writing from the publisher, except by a reviewer.

Articles in Greenhaven Publishing anthologies are often edited for length to meet page
requirements. In addition, original titles of these works are changed to clearly present
the main thesis and to explicitly indicate the author's opinion. Every effort is made to
ensure that Greenhaven Publishing accurately reflects the original intent of the authors.
Every effort has been made to trace the owners of the copyrighted material.

Cover image: Brendan Bannon/AFP/Getty Images
Map: frees/Shutterstock.com

Library of Congress Cataloging-in-Publication Data

Names: Lusted, Marcia Amidon, editor.
Title: Climate change and population displacement / Marcia Amidon Lusted,
  book editor.
Description: New York : Greenhaven Publishing, [2020] | Series: Global
  viewpoints | Audience: Grades 9 to 12. | Includes bibliographical
  references and index.
Identifiers: LCCN 2018058992 | ISBN 9781534505544 (library bound) | ISBN
  9781534505551 (pbk.)
Subjects: LCSH: Population—Environmental aspects—Juvenile literature. |
  Environmental refugees—Juvenile literature. | Climatic changes—Economic
  aspects—Juvenile literature.
Classification: LCC HB849.415 C55 2019 | DDC 362.87—dc23
LC record available at https://lccn.loc.gov/2018058992

Manufactured in the United States of America

Website: http://greenhavenpublishing.com

Contents

Chapter 1: Climate Change and Population Displacement Around the World

Chapter 2: The Causes and Effects of Climate Change Migration

Chapter 3: The Politics of Climate Change

Chapter 4: An Uneasy Future

Foreword

*"The problems of all of humanity can
only be solved by all of humanity."*
—Swiss author Friedrich Dürrenmatt

Global interdependence has become an undeniable reality. Mass media and technology have increased worldwide access to information and created a society of global citizens. Understanding and navigating this global community is a challenge, requiring a high degree of information literacy and a new level of learning sophistication.

Building on the success of its flagship series, Opposing Viewpoints, Greenhaven Publishing has created the Global Viewpoints series to examine a broad range of current, often-controversial topics of worldwide importance from a variety of international perspectives. Providing students and other readers with the information they need to explore global connections and think critically about worldwide implications, each Global Viewpoints volume offers a panoramic view of a topic of widespread significance.

Drugs, famine, immigration—a broad, international treatment is essential to do justice to social, environmental, health, and political issues such as these. Junior high, high school, and early college students, as well as general readers, can all use Global Viewpoints anthologies to discern the complexities relating to each issue. Readers will be able to examine unique national perspectives while, at the same time, appreciating the interconnectedness that global priorities bring to all nations and cultures.

Material in each volume is selected from a diverse range of sources, including journals, magazines, newspapers, nonfiction books, speeches, government documents, pamphlets, organization newsletters, and position papers. Global Viewpoints is truly global, with material drawn primarily from international sources available in English and secondarily from US sources with extensive international coverage.

Features of each volume in the Global Viewpoints series include:

- An **annotated table of contents** that provides a brief summary of each essay in the volume, including the name of the country or area covered in the essay.

- An **introduction** specific to the volume topic.

- A world map to help readers locate the countries or areas covered in the essays.

- For each viewpoint, an **introduction** that contains notes about the author and source of the viewpoint explains why material from the specific country is being presented, summarizes the main points of the viewpoint, and offers three **guided reading questions** to aid in understanding and comprehension.

- **For further discussion** questions that promote critical thinking by asking the reader to compare and contrast aspects of the viewpoints or draw conclusions about perspectives and arguments.

- A worldwide list of **organizations to contact** for readers seeking additional information.

- A **periodical bibliography** for each chapter and a **bibliography of books** on the volume topic to aid in further research.

- A comprehensive **subject index** to offer access to people, places, events, and subjects cited in the text.

Global Viewpoints is designed for a broad spectrum of readers who want to learn more about current events, history, political science, government, international relations, economics, environmental science, world cultures, and sociology—students doing research for class assignments or debates, teachers and faculty seeking to supplement course materials, and others wanting to understand current issues better. By presenting how people in various countries perceive the root causes, current consequences, and proposed solutions to worldwide challenges, Global Viewpoints volumes offer readers opportunities to enhance their global awareness and their knowledge of cultures worldwide.

Introduction

"Between 2008 and 2015, an average of 26.4 million people per year were displaced by climate- or weather-related disasters, according to the United Nations. And the science of climate change indicates that these trends are likely to get worse."[1]

Almost every day, the news has at least one story about extreme weather events, disasters, unusual weather, melting polar ice caps, and many other stories that have to do with the increasingly serious problem of climate change. From frequent catastrophic wildfires in California, to hurricanes that are more common and more powerful than ever before, to droughts that cause starvation in many countries, the changing climate is having violent and devastating effects. Climate change itself has been a controversial topic: Does it really exist? Are unpredictable and more extreme weather events due to human-influenced climate change, or simply part of a natural cycle of the earth? Should governments begin planning for climate change and cooperating to establish guidelines and policies to deal with it?

Most scientists now believe that climate change is real, and that it is no longer an unproven theory. It is the result of man-made causes, such as the use of fossil fuels for generating energy, fueling cars, and heating homes. Many of the effects of climate change are already being seen; according to the Union of Concerned Scientists, the global sea level has risen 8 inches since the year 1880, and it is rising even faster on the East Coast of the United States and the Gulf of Mexico. Higher spring and summer temperatures and the corresponding earlier snow melt are fueling more wildfires in the western United States. In India, dangerous heat waves are killing people. Storms are dumping more and more precipitation, in short violent storms that make it difficult to deal with excessive snow or rain and result in flooding or in snow depths that paralyze normal services like transportation and energy.

Scientist also warn that there is the potential for an abrupt climate change, which Earth has experienced in the past. A shift in the circulation pattern of the ocean could have drastic consequences for Europe and the United States. A changed climate could affect the food chain of plants and animals and alter habitats and ranges.

However, climate change isn't just about weather, climate, and changing seasons. It is also making some parts of the world more and more hostile. In some African countries that are undergoing extreme drought, people can no longer grow enough food to feed themselves, or access enough water to survive. Some Pacific island nations are disappearing under rising sea levels, forcing inhabitants to leave. Areas experiencing extreme cold or extreme heat may soon be uninhabitable. Climate refugees—people who are forced to flee their homes because they can no longer survive there—are becoming more common. The Environmental Justice Foundation estimates that by the year 2050, there could be 150 million climate refugees. Not only will these refugees need to find new places to live but political strife will increase as governments try to decide where refugees can settle and where they are not welcome. Political conflict could well increase, as well as conflict between people, households, towns, cities, and within countries themselves.

It is going to become increasingly important for countries to not only negotiate treaties and other formal systems for handling climate refugees but also to begin enacting policies and laws to try to slow the rate of climate change and its effects. It is also going to become very important for all people, no matter where they live in the world and what their climates might currently be, to do whatever they can do on a personal level to reduce their carbon footprints and try to reduce some of the causes of climate change in their daily lives.

The perspectives in *Global Viewpoints: Climate Change and Population Displacement* explore this interesting and developing issue. Climate change is affecting everyone, all over the globe, and whether or not a person finds himself or herself in the position of becoming a climate refugee or victim of extreme weather, everyone will need to work together to save the people, plants, animals, oceans, and landscapes of the planet.

[1]Gulrez Shah Azhar, "Climate change could displace up to 300 million people by 2050," The Conversation, December 25, 2017.

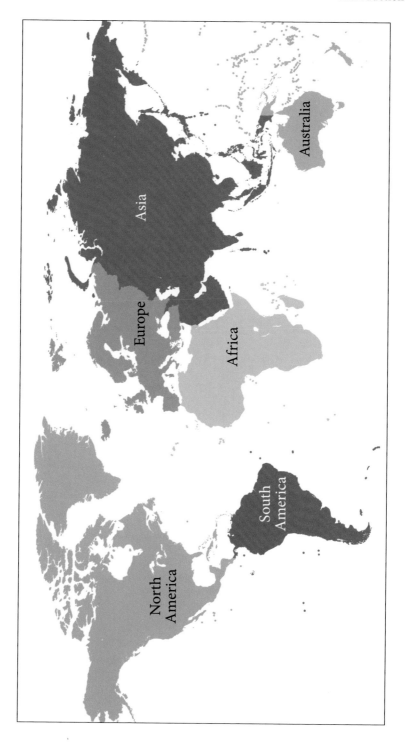

GLOBALVIEWPOINTS

CHAPTER 1

Climate Change and Population Displacement Around the World

Summer Heat Waves Were a Sign

Bob Berwyn

In the following viewpoint, Bob Berwyn presents evidence of warming trends during the summer of 2018 and how they are related to climate change. He discusses how these temperatures are affecting infrastructure, food security, and human well-being, and suggests they are a warning sign of things to come as the climate changes. Berwyn also suggests about what needs to be done immediately to address these growing concerns. Berwyn is an environmental journalist and a contributing writer for Pacific Standard.

As you read, consider the following questions:

1. According to the article, what are some of the specific results of warming global temperatures?
2. How are some basic elements of infrastructure being affected by heat?
3. How does the jet stream affect global temperatures?

Earth's global warming fever spiked to deadly new highs across the Northern Hemisphere this summer, and we're feeling the results—extreme heat is now blamed for hundreds of deaths, droughts threaten food supplies, wildfires have raced through neighborhoods in the western United States, Greece and as far north as the Arctic Circle.

"This Summer's Heat Waves Could Be the Strongest Climate Signal Yet," by Bob Berwyn, Inside Climate News, July 28, 2018. Reprinted by permission.

At sea, record and near-record warm oceans have sent soggy masses of air surging landward, fueling extreme rainfall and flooding in Japan and the eastern US. In Europe, the Baltic Sea is so warm that potentially toxic blue-green algae is spreading across its surface.

There shouldn't be any doubt that some of the deadliest of this summer's disasters—including flooding in Japan and wildfires in Greece—are fueled by weather extremes linked to global warming, said Corinne Le Quéré, director of the Tyndall Centre for Climate Change Research at the University of East Anglia.

"We know very well that global warming is making heat waves longer, hotter and more frequent," she said.

"The evidence from having extreme events around the world is really compelling. It's very indicative that the global warming background is causing or at least contributing to these events," she said.

The challenges created by global warming are becoming evident even in basic infrastructure, much of which was built on the assumption of a cooler climate. In these latest heat waves, railroad tracks have bent in the rising temperatures, airport runways have cracked, and power plants from France to Finland have had to power down because their cooling sources became too warm.

"We're seeing that many things are not built to withstand the heat levels we are seeing now," Le Quéré said.

Penn State climate scientist Michael Mann said this summer's extreme weather fits into a pattern he identified with other researchers in a study published last year. The jet stream's north-south meanders have been unusually stationary, leading to persistent heat waves and droughts in some areas and days of rain and flooding in others, he said. "Our work last year shows that this sort of pattern ... has become more common because of human-caused climate change, and in particular, amplified Arctic warming."

Deadly Heat Waves from Canada to Japan

There are many ways to define a heat wave, but the conditions in many areas of the planet this summer have been universally recognized as severe, said Boram Lee, a senior research scientist with the World Meteorological Organization.

"From around end of June, many countries in Europe, Asia and North America have issued severe warnings," she said. The UK, US, Japan and Korea all had long-lasting warnings, and Japan declared the recent heat wave a natural disaster, she added.

In Europe, scientists on Friday released a real-time attribution study of the heat wave that has baked parts of northern Europe since June. They found that global warming caused by greenhouse gas pollution made the ongoing heat wave five times more likely in Denmark, and twice as likely in Ireland.

"Near the Arctic, it's absolutely exceptional and unprecedented. This is a warning," said French heat wave expert Robert Vautard, who worked on the study for World Weather Attribution. The group previously determined that global warming made last summer's "Lucifer" heat wave in southern Europe 10 times more likely.

"In many places, people are preparing for the past or present climate. But this summer is the future," he said.

The geographic scope and persistence of the European heat wave stands out. An area stretching from the British Isles to Eastern Europe and north to the Arctic is bright red on European heat wave and drought maps, covering an area about as big as Texas and California combined.

Crop damage is being reported in parts of Norway through Sweden, Denmark and the Baltics. Depending on conditions during the next month, more widespread crop failures could raise global food prices.

In mid-July, temperatures reached all-time record highs above the Arctic Circle, around 90 degrees Fahrenheit, and hovered in the 80s for weeks at a time. In the Norwegian glacier area that Lars Holger Pilø studies, the average temperature has been 9 degrees Fahrenheit above average for the past 30 days.

"I have been working here since 2006, and we have snow records going back 60 years, and there's nothing like what we're seeing right now," said Pilø, part of a team of ice archaeologists who are measuring the snow and ice loss and recovering historic artifacts like arrowheads and skis that were buried for millennia.

"I'm watching with a mixture of excitement and dread. I try not to think too much about it and stick to what we do, which is rescuing the artifacts coming out of the warming. I call it dark archaeology," he said. "I look at the ice and I think, dead man walking."

Norwegian Meteorological Institute climate scientist Ketil Isaksen said the extreme situation in Scandinavia fits with the pattern of global warming.

"There are so many extremes now from all over the world. We're seeing a very common pattern. For me this is a strong climate signal. Ice that's several thousand years old, melting in the matter of just a few weeks," he said.

Isaksen is finalizing some studies that find heat is penetrating between 30 and 50 meters deep into the ground through cracks in the rocky mountains around Norway's fjords. Instead of just a thin skin of permafrost melting, those mountains could fall apart in large chunks when autumn rains start, threatening coastal communities with tsunamis.

"Now we have a new extreme this summer. This will probably affect slope stability, and we can expect mass movement events like debris flows and landslides in late summer," he said.

He said the studies help define new geologic hazard areas with knowledge that some of the melted mountains will see wholesale slope failure when strong rains hit. Based on the information, emergency managers are developing new early warning systems.

The Increasing Influence of Global Warming

About the same time the Norwegian researchers were uncovering ancient tools in the Arctic tundra this summer, heat records were being set in many other parts of the world.

Temperatures in Algeria reached 124 degrees Fahrenheit, setting a record for the African continent. A few weeks earlier, a city in Oman is believed to have broken a global record when it went more than 24 hours with temperatures never falling below 108 degrees. Japan set a national record of 106 amid a heat wave that has been blamed for more than 80 deaths.

Regional western heat events are becoming so pronounced that some climate scientists see the current extremes in the US as a climate inflection point, where the global warming signal stands out above the natural background of climate variability.

In mid-July, a week of temperatures in the high 80s and up to 96 degrees Fahrenheit in normally cool Quebec killed more than 50 people, and while that heat wave was waning, another was building in Asia, where the Japan Meteorological Agency said that 200 of its 927 stations topped the 35 degree Celsius (95 degrees Fahrenheit) on July 15. Since then, at least 80 people have died and thousands have gone to hospitals with heat-related ailments.

"There are irrefutable scientific evidences that climate change alters both the intensity and frequency of such extreme phenomena as heat waves, and ongoing efforts are dedicated to understand how big the impact of man-made climate change is," said the WMO's Boram Lee.

Across social media, climate scientists are responding with a collective "we warned about this," posting links to 10 years' worth of studies that have consistently been projecting increases in deadly heat waves. If anything, the warnings may have been understated.

"The rise in heat waves is stronger than many climate models project," said World Weather Attribution's Geert Jan van Oldenborgh, who measured a record high temperature outside his office in the Netherlands on July 26, then tweeted that global warming is making the heat there 20 times more likely than in 1900.

Wildfires Out of Control

Hot and dry weather also makes forests more flammable. In Greece, after a month of record and near-record heat, flames ran wild through the community of Mati on July 23, killing at least 80 people. On July 26, a blaze in Northern California jumped the Sacramento River and spawned fire tornadoes, forcing the evacuation of parts of Redding, a city of 92,000. And in Germany, residents of southern Berlin awoke Friday to the sight of smoke on the horizon, an event that will also become more common in that part of the world.

Although climate scientists are reluctant to link any one particular fire to climate change, there is plenty of scientific evidence showing how heat-trapping greenhouse gases contribute to increased fire danger.

"Weather is a product of the climate system. We are drastically altering that system, and all the weather we observe now is the product of that human-altered climate system. One result is an increase in the frequency, size and severity of large fire events," University of California, Merced researcher Leroy Westerling wrote on Twitter.

University of Arizona climate researcher and geographer Kevin Anchukaitis publicized several wildfire studies from the last 10 years that all show how and why global warming is making fires bigger, more destructive and longer-lasting. "Is climate change the only factor influencing wildland fire? No, of course not—but climate change is influencing area burned and fuel aridity," he wrote.

Tyndall Centre Director Le Quéré said she faulted some media for failing to connect global warming to the current global heat wave. "This signal is very clear," she said, adding that some of the early stories about the deadly fire in Greece almost seemed to downplay a link to climate change.

On Friday, the WMO released a new statement highlighting the links between global warming and wildfires and reminding readers that "heat is drying out forests and making them more susceptible to burn."

Extreme Rainfall and Flooding

There is also still reluctance to link individual extreme flood events with global warming, despite plenty of scientific evidence that today's global atmosphere—1 degree Celsius warmer than 100 years

Is Climate Change Always to Blame for Extreme Weather?

When the news is full of stories on extreme weather, it's hard not to wonder: Is this what climate change looks like?

Climate scientists say yes—though it's complicated.

Take wildfires, for example. "We see five times more large fires today than we did in the 1970s," says Jennifer Balch, professor in geography and director of Earth Lab at the University of Colorado Boulder.

Wildfires are part of the ecosystem of the American West, and scientists expect a certain number of them under normal average conditions. But what global warming does, says Balch, is change the backdrop against which they happen.

"Fire season is about three months longer than it was just a few decades ago," she says. Last year was the costliest fire season ever, with damages exceeding $18 billion.

Overall, weather and climate disasters in the US caused more than $300 billion in damages in 2017, shattering previous records. Though that's not all climate—those increased costs are partly the result of development and sprawl.

Andreas Prein is a research scientist at the National Center for Atmospheric Research in Boulder, Colorado. "What we see from climate change is that you lose a lot of these very moderate and light rainfall storms and replace it with very intense storms," he says. Over the last 50 years, the number of really big rainstorms has increased by as much as 70 percent.

Some aspects of climate change are pretty certain, he says. Temperatures are rising. Rainstorms and heat waves are getting more intense. These are the long-predicted results of increased greenhouse gas emissions.

To a certain degree, that we've had so much extreme weather this past week is a coincidence: fires, heat waves, and rainstorms happen every summer. But climate change makes this kind of extreme weather more common, researchers say—and it's a trend that's expected to continue as the planet keeps getting warmer.

"When the Weather Is Extreme, Is Climate Change to Blame?"
by Laurel Wamsley, NPR.org, July 29, 2018

ago—holds much more moisture that can be delivered by regional storm systems.

Those warnings were not enough to help the more than 200 people who died in Japan in late June amid a series of record-setting torrential rain storms. Regional weather patterns certainly played a role, but ocean currents and an atmosphere juiced up by global warming likely boosted moisture for the storm.

Two years ago, Alfred Wegener Institute climate researcher Hu Yang showed how climate change is strengthening ocean currents that carry moisture from the ocean toward Japan. The research showed the currents have been getting stronger and warmer in tandem with rising atmospheric CO2 levels. Eventually, that heat is released to the atmosphere during storms, as wind or rain or both.

Yang said his continuing research is finding similar evidence that a powerful current near Japan may be "a super hotspot under global warming." As the current strengthens, it will release its energy as water vapor, fuel for storms that can cause extra heavy rains in Japan and other parts of Asia, he said.

In the US, June flooding in the Midwest fits a detected pattern of increasing extreme rainfalls in that region. And in late July, 10 million people in the East, from Pennsylvania to North Carolina, were under various types of flood warnings with soggy air sloshing from the Gulf of Mexico and the Caribbean over the overheated Northeastern Atlantic toward the coast.

What Can We Do About It?

In some cases, the scientific warnings about global warming impacts have resonated. At least parts of Europe are better prepared for heat waves now than they were in 2003, when extreme heat killed up to 70,000 people, said Le Quéré.

More cities know what they need to do to protect vulnerable people in an extreme event, she said, but they lack the money to do things like building more cooling shelters, or cooling core urban areas with green spaces and ponds.

"Maybe this is an opportunity, in a grim way, to prepare for events that will be longer and hotter," she said. "It's not just a case of holding our breath for three weeks and saying 'it's soon winter.' It's a time to push and protect vulnerable people and infrastructure."

To prepare for the new normal, people must act in the next five to 10 years, said environmental scientist Cara Augustenborg, chairperson of Friends of the Earth Europe.

"We have to consider how every new infrastructure, agricultural or development project from now on will be impacted by climate change. We need to look at planned retreat from coastlines and developing further inland, building infrastructure that is more resilient to the effects of climate change such as sea level rise and temperature extremes.

"We've had several years now where airport runways have melted on extremely hot days," she continued. "That's something we need to factor in to future construction as it's a problem that won't go away."

Society also needs to think about food security, she said.

"That's what I really lose sleep over," she said. "Our available arable land is declining now as our global population is booming. It doesn't take much in the way of extreme weather to have a major impact on food supplies."

In Japan a Tsunami Led to a Nuclear Plant Disaster

Bill Dawson

The news media has always reported on extreme weather events such as storms, earthquakes, and heat and cold waves. In recent years, disasters and weather events related to climate change have begun to dominate news coverage. In the following viewpoint, Bill Dawson highlights some of the disaster and weather coverage of recent months, especially concerning four major events with causes that can be traced to the changing weather systems and climate change. Dawson is assistant editor at the Society of Environmental Journalists' SEJournal.

As you read, consider the following questions:

1. What questions arose from the Japanese tsunami?
2. What conflict has resulted from the drought and fires in Texas?
3. Why are experts undecided about the link between climate change and the number of tornadoes?

D isasters drive news coverage. Well, yes, that's not exactly an insightfully original observation. Dogs also chase cats. Night follows day. Editors cut stories.

"Enterprising Stories Stand Out in Recent Disaster Coverage — From Japan to Texas," by Bill Dawson, The Society of Environmental Journalists, July 15, 2011. Reprinted by permission.

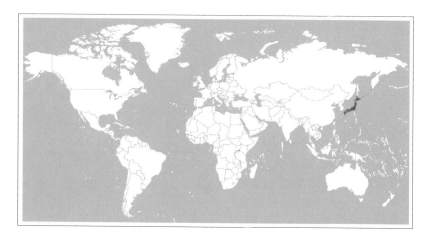

Still, any examination or cataloging of environmental coverage has to deal with the central place of disasters on the environment beat.

The names of some iconic events—Three Mile Island, Chernobyl, Bhopal, Exxon Valdez—echo down through the years in follow-up coverage, anniversary coverage, coverage of seemingly never-ending policy debates and lawsuits.

Disasters and extreme weather have once again had a prominent place in environmental reporting in recent months, so The Beat this time takes note of a sampling of that coverage.

In particular, we focus on a few of the many enterprise stories that emanated from four clusters of events—the tsunami-caused crisis at Japan's Fukushima nuclear plant, drought and wildfires in Texas, death-dealing tornadoes in the Southeast and massive flooding in the Mississippi River system.

Fukushima

Possible safety lessons provided a major focus for coverage after a March 11 earthquake launched the tsunami that crippled emergency generators needed to cool the Japanese nuclear plant's reactors.

Mike Soraghan of Greenwire reported on March 24, for instance, on the debate about whether backup power at most US nuclear plants—batteries required to last four hours—is sufficient.

On April 9, Todd B. Bates of New Jersey's *Asbury Park Press* reported that his investigation had revealed "millions of gallons of radioactive water have leaked from nuclear power plants throughout the US since the 1970s, threatening water supplies in New Jersey and other states."

Two months after the earthquake, the results of such journalistic inquiries were continuing to be unveiled.

On May 11, Susan Q. Stranahan reported for iWatch News (the newly rebranded website of the investigative Center for Public Integrity) that fires are "nuclear power's more probable threat," but typically bring only "slaps on the wrist" from the Nuclear Regulatory Commission (NRC).

In an article from Tokyo on May 2, AP staff writers Yuri Kageyama and Justin Pritchard reported that their in-depth review of "Japan's approach to nuclear plant safety shows how closely intertwined relationships between government regulators and industry have allowed a culture of complacency to prevail."

Also with a Tokyo dateline, the *New York Times*' Norimitsu Onishi and James Glanz had reported on March 26 that "in the country that gave the world the word tsunami, the Japanese nuclear establishment largely disregarded the potentially destructive force of the walls of water."

On April 12, Michail Hengtensberg, Gensche Sager and Philline Gebhardt, reporting for Spiegel Online, produced a detailed "survey of the world's radioactive no-go zones," observing that this "look at some of the worst incidents is enough to demonstrate just how high the price of nuclear energy and nuclear weapons truly is."

Taking off from US officials' call for Americans within 50 miles of the Japanese reactors to evacuate, *Mother Jones*' Kate Sheppard on March 22 examined the NRC's current 10-mile evacuation zone around US plants. A chart listed dozens of US cities within a 50-mile radius of reactors.

Five days before Sheppard's story was posted, Bill Dedman of MSNBC had reported that the NRC's new earthquake-risk calculations show the highest risk not at some California reactor near the San Andreas Fault.

It is, he reported, at the Indian Point Energy Center, 24 miles north of New York City—a 1-in-10,000 chance of damage to the reactor core each year, or "right on the verge of requiring 'immediate concern regarding adequate protection' of the public."

Drought and Fire

Did the spring's drought-associated rash of Texas wildfires officially constitute a disaster? Texas and federal officials were still disagreeing at the time this column was written. (The feds said no.)

Were the drought and fires in Texas a symptom of man-made climate change? Journalists weighed in on that issue, just as they did in regard to the destructive tornadoes and flooding along the Mississippi.

Randy Lee Loftis of the Dallas Morning News addressed the question head-on in a story on April 16, asking whether, besides La Nina ("the immediate cause," in scientists' estimation), "the drought and fires [were] also linked to climate change."

Loftis's answer: "Climate scientists say that question, though common whenever extreme weather arrives, is both unanswerable and misdirected." He added: "Most climate models—projections of future conditions from supercomputers processing huge amounts of data—say Texas will get less rainfall as global temperatures keep rising."

In an April 27 blog post that, like Loftis's story, prominently quoted Texas state climatologist John Nielsen-Gammon, the Houston Chronicle's Eric Berger jabbed a local environmentalist for "scare-mongering" because the advocate had written his own blog post for the Chronicle, noting that "people starved to death during the Dust Bowl days" and that "Gaia creator James Lovelock has said that by 2100 there will be about 1 billion people on Earth, the other 6 billion or so having starved to death."

Texas Tribune reporter Kate Galbraith had a story on April 21, co-published in the *New York Times*, about how the West Texas oil city Midland was grappling with its dwindling water supply. Discussion of climate change only appeared in a shorter, associated blog post in the *Times* the next day.

The blog item also quoted Nielsen-Gammon: "Certainly global warming has contributed to the rate at which the ground has dried out because of the warm temperatures, [but] the magnitude of the dryness is well beyond what global warming would be able to do so far."

It also included comments by the Midland mayor, an "oilman," who said, in Galbraith's paraphrase, that "reducing carbon dioxide emissions seems like the right thing to do for the long term, taking into account future generations."

Deadly Tornadoes

April's record-setting number of tornadoes likewise drew attention to the possible link to global warming. Here are some examples of coverage that addressed the question with due caution about current scientific understanding.

A story on April 25 by the *Times*' A. G. Sulzberger: "Though scientists believe that climate change will contribute to increasingly severe weather phenomena, including hurricanes and thunderstorms, there is little consensus about how it may affect tornadoes."

Similarly, in a longer article on April 28 by the same newspaper's Kirk Johnson: "The prevalence of hurricanes, droughts and floods has been linked in many climate models to the impact of a warming planet. Such a connection is more tentative when it comes to twisters."

Stephanie Pappas of LiveScience.com on the same day: "Some climate models suggest that a warming future could herald more intense storms like those that ripped through the Southeast on Wednesday night. But that doesn't mean the southern storms and tornadoes were a manifestation of climate change, climate scientists say. That's because teasing out the influence of climate on weather takes time."

Also on April 28, the Toronto Star's Mitch Potter: "While a raft of climate science points to a stormier future involving more frequent and possibly more severe hurricanes, researchers have yet to factor tornadoes into climate-change predictions with any certainty."

The *Los Angeles Times'* Eryn Brown on April 29, quoting Chris Weiss, an atmospheric science professor at Texas Tech University: "The role of global warming in the phenomenon is unclear," he [said], noting that it's hard to relate individual weather events to the long-term sweep of climate change, and that even if one could, there's "significant debate" in the scientific literature about whether warming will increase or decrease the number of tornadoes.

Ferris Jabr in New Scientist on May 3: "Climate change cannot be directly blamed for such outbreaks [like the Southeast's thunderstorms and tornadoes]. And even as scientists' climate models have improved, the question of whether increasing global temperatures will change the frequency and severity of dangerous weather in the future remains open."

Editor's Note: Not long after this column was submitted, even more deadly tornadoes hit Oklahoma and Missouri. Most notably, the Joplin, Mo., tornado leveled a third of the town of 50,000 residents, killing at least 140 persons. It prompted President Obama to visit the devastated city in late May and helped make 2011 the most deadly year for tornadoes on record. Check an upcoming *SEJournal* for more on the media's tornado coverage.

Mississippi River

Once again, the issue of climate change was placed in the spotlight by some journalists as the mammoth flood crest on the Mississippi moved southward toward the Gulf of Mexico.

In an installment broadcast the week of May 6, Public Radio International's "Living on Earth" program interviewed Weather Underground co-founder Jeff Masters about the possible climate change connection to flooding on the Mississippi and its largest tributary the Ohio River, as well as the tornado outbreak.

Bruce Gellerman asked Masters "how bad [flooding in the area] could get, say, in 90 years—2100."

A projected 20 percent rainfall increase over the Mississippi Valley could mean even more flooding, he replied: "The thought is it would increase runoff by more like 50 percent. Because what happens when you start getting heavier rains is now you've got a saturated soil that can't absorb rain anymore—so you tend to get more runoff."

In an "explainer" posted May 11, Climate Central managing editor Andrew Freedman reported that climate change can't be blamed for causing this year's flooding. He added:

"Scientists are working to detect the 'fingerprint' of global warming in specific extreme weather events, and their methods are still in their infancy. It will take many months for studies to be completed on whether climate change may have made April's heavy rains more likely. For now, though, we can look at studies that have already been completed that offer some clues about the relationship between climate change and heavy precipitation events."

Ned Potter of ABC News, meanwhile, discussed the matter of flood-borne pollutants and contaminants in a piece that was web-posted on May 11:

"ABC News arranged some testing of its own, taking water samples from two places along the river to a laboratory near Memphis. E. coli and coliform—commonly found in untreated waste water—were 2,000 times acceptable limits. The lab did not find gasoline, oil or chemical toxins. There were trace levels of heavy metals, but no more than would be found ordinarily, the lab reported."

The day before, on May 10, NPR's Scott Neuman related some pertinent historical context about the current floods in a piece entitled "Along the Mississippi, an old sense of dread arises."

He reported:

"The flooding has prompted comparisons to the Great Flood of 1927—a catastrophe that riveted the nation's attention, spurred demands for government action and ultimately changed how Americans think about natural disasters.

"A year later, Congress passed the Flood Control Act of 1928, which authorized the US Army Corps of Engineers to design and construct a system of levees and spillways to control flooding on the Mississippi River and its tributaries."

In Africa and Asia the Coastal Poor Are Being Pushed to the Most Dangerous Zones for Climate Change

The World Bank Group

In the following viewpoint the World Bank Group argues that climate change and the resulting population displacement could ultimately affect many parts of the world, but the effects of a changing climate are already impacting places in Africa and Asia much more than other areas of the world, specifically the poorer populations who live there. Low-lying areas are being increasingly affected by flooding, and other areas are experiencing droughts that are impacting water supplies and the ability to grow food. The World Bank Group is a global partnership that works to end extreme poverty and promote shared prosperity.

As you read, consider the following questions:

1. Why are these areas especially vulnerable to climate change?
2. What could some of the effects be of just a degree or two in global temperature?
3. How do warmer ocean temperatures and acidity affect coral reefs?

"What Climate Change Means for Africa, Asia and the Coastal Poor," The World Bank Group, June 19, 2013. Reprinted by permission.

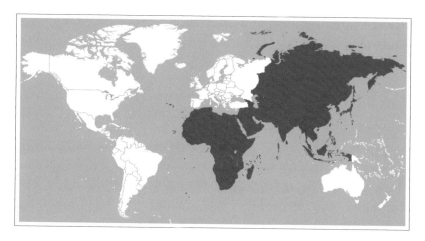

As the coastal cities of Africa and Asia expand, many of their poorest residents are being pushed to the edges of livable land and into the most dangerous zones for climate change. Their informal settlements cling to riverbanks and cluster in low-lying areas with poor drainage, few public services, and no protection from storm surges, sea-level rise, and flooding.

These communities—the poor in coastal cities and on low-lying islands—are among the world's most vulnerable to climate change and the least able to marshal the resources to adapt, a new report finds. They face a world where climate change will increasingly threaten the food supplies of Sub-Saharan Africa and the farm fields and water resources of South Asia and South East Asia within the next three decades, while extreme weather puts their homes and lives at risk.

A new scientific report commissioned by the World Bank and released on June 19 explores the risks to lives and livelihoods in these three highly vulnerable regions. Turn Down the Heat: Climate Extremes, Regional Impacts, and the Case for Resilience (Read it in Issuu, Scribd, Open Knowledge Repository) takes the climate discussion to the next level, building on a 2012 World Bank report that concluded from a global perspective that without a clear mitigation strategy and effort, the world is headed for average temperatures 4 degrees Celsius warmer than pre-industrial times by the end of this century.

Small Number, Big Problem

Communities around the world are already feeling the impacts of climate change today, with the planet only 0.8°C warmer than in pre-industrial times. Many of us could experience the harsher impacts of a 2°C warmer world within our lifetimes—20 to 30 years from now—and 4°C is likely by the end of the century without global action.

The report lays out what these temperature increases will look like, degree-by-degree, in each targeted region and the damage anticipated for agricultural production, coastal cities, and water resources.

"The scientists tell us that if the world warms by 2°C—warming which may be reached in 20 to 30 years—that will cause widespread food shortages, unprecedented heat-waves, and more intense cyclones," said World Bank Group President Jim Yong Kim. "In the near-term, climate change, which is already unfolding, could batter the slums even more and greatly harm the lives and the hopes of individuals and families who have had little hand in raising the Earth's temperature."

The report, based on scientific analysis by the Potsdam Institute for Climate Impact Research and Climate Analytics, uses advanced computer simulations to paint the clearest picture of each region's vulnerabilities. It describes the risks to agriculture and livelihood security in Sub-Saharan Africa; the rise in sea-level, loss of coral reefs and devastation to coastal areas likely in South East Asia; and the fluctuating water resources in South Asia that can lead to flooding in some areas and water scarcity in others, as well as affecting power supply.

"The second phase of this report truly reiterates our need to bring global attention to the tasks necessary to hold warming to 2°C," said Rachel Kyte, the Bank's vice president for sustainable development. "Our ideas at the World Bank have already been put into practice as we move forward to assist those whose lives are particularly affected by extreme weather events."

Sub-Saharan Africa

In Sub-Saharan Africa, the researchers found food security will be the overarching challenge, with dangers from droughts, flooding, and shifts in rainfall.

Between 1.5°C and 2°C warming, drought and aridity will contribute to farmers losing 40–80 percent of cropland conducive to growing maize, millet, and sorghum by the 2030s–2040s, the researchers found.

In a 4°C warmer world, around the 2080s, annual precipitation may decrease by up to 30 percent in southern Africa, while East Africa will see more rainfall, according to multiple studies. Ecosystem changes to pastoral lands, such as a shift from grass to woodland savannas as levels of carbon dioxide increase, could reduce food for grazing cattle.

South East Asia

In South East Asia, coastal cities will be under intense stress due to climate change.

A sea-level rise of 30 cm, possible by 2040 if business as usual continues, would cause massive flooding in cities and inundate low-lying cropland with saltwater corrosive to crops. Vietnam's Mekong Delta, a global rice producer, is particularly vulnerable to sea-level rise. A 30 cm sea-level rise there could result in the loss of about 11 percent of crop production. At the same time, storm intensity is likely to increase.

The study also describes rising ocean acidity leading to the loss of coral reefs and the benefits they provide as fish habitats, protection against storms, and revenue-generators in the form of tourism. Warmer water temperatures and habitat destruction could also lead to a 50 percent decrease in the ocean fish catch in the southern Philippines, the report says.

South Asia

Water scarcity in some areas and overabundance of water in others are the hallmarks of climate change in South Asia, the researchers found.

Inconsistences in the monsoon season and unusual heat extremes will affect crops. Loss of snow melt from the Himalayas will reduce the flow of water into the Indus, Ganges and Brahmaputra basins. Together, they threaten to leave hundreds of millions of people without enough water, food, or access to reliable energy. Bangladesh and the Indian cities of Kolkata and Mumbai will be confronted with increased flooding, intense cyclones, sea-level rise, and warming temperatures.

World Bank's Response

In his first year as president of the World Bank, Jim Kim has raised the profile of climate change in speeches and in conversations with leaders around the world, as well as within the institution. The Bank is currently working with 130 countries on climate change; it doubled its lending for adaptation to $4.6 billion in 2012 and put $7.1 billion into mitigation, in addition to its work with carbon finance and the Climate Investment Funds; and it now includes climate change in all country assessments.

The Bank is also developing a Climate Management Action Plan, informed by the Turn Down the Heat reports, to direct its future work and finance through a climate lens. Among other things, the Bank will:

- Help countries develop strategic plans and investment pipelines that integrate the risks and opportunities of climate change.

- Provide the tools that countries and cities need to better assess and adapt to climate change, including greenhouse gas emissions tracking, energy use and efficiency assessments, and assessments of resilience.

- Create best practices and norms through its projects for making infrastructure resilient, not just today but decades into the future.

- Use its convening power, financial leverage and targeted climate funds to increase support for clean energy, low-carbon development, and climate resilience.

In order to help countries build resilience, the Bank will prioritize the most vulnerable areas, manage water availability and extremes, and increase its efforts to meet growing food demand. It will work with the world's largest emitters to lower their impact through carbon emissions and short-lived climate pollutants. Its specialists are working on ways to help governments end fossil fuel subsidies while protecting the poor, connect global carbon markets, and make agriculture and cities climate-smart and resilient.

"I do not believe the poor are condemned to the future scientists envision in this report," Kim said. "We are determined to work with countries to find solutions."

In Fiji a Government Responded to a Community Severely Affected by Climate Change

Michael Traeger, Raveena Grace, Maddison Brian, and Jack Simkin, with Dr. Celia McMichael

In the following viewpoint Michael Traeger, Raveena Grace, Maddison Brian, and Jack Simkin with Dr. Celia McMichael argue that as the effects of climate change become more and more real, people in some of the poorest areas of the world, such as Fiji, are being forced to leave their homes and seek new places to live, simply to survive. And yet, many countries that will feel the impact of these climate refugees seem reluctant to address the issue and develop policies for handling these new types of refugees. They must develop plans for handling the coming crisis, as more areas of the world become uninhabitable. Traeger, Grace, Brian, and Simkin are masters students at the University of Melbourne. They wrote this article as part of their coursework for the subject Science Communication.

As you read, consider the following questions:

1. What did the village of Vunidogoloa do in 2014?
2. What did Fiji's government do for those affected by coastal erosion and flooding?
3. Why is climate finance a high priority for places like Fiji?

"The Future of Climate Refugees," by Michael Traeger, Raveena Grace, Maddison Brian, and Jack Simkin with Dr. Celia McMichael. This article was first published on Pursuit. https://pursuit.unimelb.edu.au/articles/the-future-of-climate-refugees. Licensed under CC BY-ND 3.0 AU.

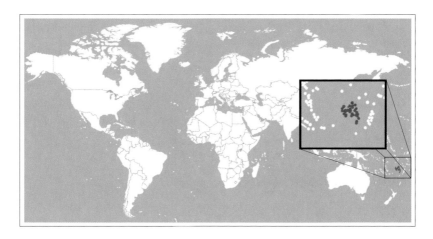

As climate change causes sea levels to rise, vulnerable populations in countries like Tuvalu, Bangladesh and Vietnam are threatened with the very real prospect of losing their homes and migrating inland.

In some places, like Fiji, this is happening already.

In 2014, the entire village of Vunidogoloa on Vanua Levu was forced to move to higher ground 2 kilometres inland to escape coastal erosion and regular flooding—environmental impacts that villagers and the Fiji Government attribute to climate change.

A further 80 villages have now been identified as at risk, and in need of relocation.

As President of this year's UN Climate Change Conference of Parties (COP23) in Bonn, Germany, Fiji has the opportunity to bring this plight to the world stage, and represent other Small Island Developing States facing similarly devastating situations.

Dr Celia McMichael from the University of Melbourne's School of Geography researches climate-related migration in Fiji in collaboration with local researchers. She says lower-income areas are among the most vulnerable to climate-related migration risks, including associated health risks.

"People and populations that are displaced after experiencing environmental disasters like flooding can be exposed to heightened risk of infectious disease and poor water and sanitation," she says.

"Forced migration also generates complex psychosocial impacts as people are dislocated and their everyday routines and social structures are interrupted.

"Displacement can provoke a loss of belonging and social networks; entire livelihoods and cultural practices are altered. This can lead to depression, anxiety and post-traumatic stress disorder."

The Vunidogoloa Way

One hundred and twenty people from 26 households in Vunidogoloa were relocated due to coastal erosion and flooding that damaged homes and crops. With the support of the Fijian Government and international agencies, the community has created new houses and livelihood opportunities.

Fiji is one of the first countries to introduce government-run programmes that relocate communities impacted by climate change, including those affected by sea-level rise. With plans in place to relocate 80 vulnerable populations across Fiji, lessons can be learned from the Vunidogoloa experience.

Dr McMichael says adverse health consequences can be reduced or avoided with careful management.

"Villagers, government agencies and donors are keenly aware of the need to ensure ongoing food security including small-scale farming, to build water systems that can provide sufficient potable water in sites of relocation, and to develop and maintain livelihoods particularly where they have moved away from existing jobs," says Dr McMichael.

But, she says, we need to learn more about the different aspects of climate migration and to develop international laws and frameworks to support these migrants. She adds that migration shouldn't be seen as the only adaptive approach to the consequences of climate change.

"In the Pacific and other countries, people are saying 'We're not climate refugees. We want to adapt. Migration isn't our only option'," says Dr McMichael.

Record High Displacement

One in every 113 people on the planet is now a refugee. Around the world, someone is displaced every three seconds, forced from their homes by violence, war and persecution.

By the end of 2016, the number of displaced people had risen to 65.6 million—more than the population of the United Kingdom. The number is an increase of 300,000 on the year before, and the largest number ever recorded, according to the UN Refugee Agency, UNHCR.

Refugees who have fled to another country make up the next biggest group, which at 22.5 million people is the highest number ever recorded. Predictably, Syria, now in its seventh year of conflict, is generating the highest number of refugees. Five and a half million fled the country last year. But over the course of 2016, South Sudan became a major new source of refugees after the breakdown of peace efforts in July contributed to 739,900 people crossing the border by the end of the year. Since then, the number of people who have left has climbed to 1.87 million people.

Finally, there are 2.8 million asylum seekers, refugees that have fled their own country and are seeking protection elsewhere.

Worryingly, the number of people being displaced continues to grow. Of the total refugee count in 2016, 10.3 million of them became refugees that year.

But, on a more positive note, thousands of people were able to return to their homes in 2016, and many others managed to resettle in other countries. About half a million refugees returned to their home countries, and around 6.5 million of those that had fled within their own countries were able to go back to their own region—although many did in less than ideal circumstances and face an uncertain future.

"The number of displaced people in the world just hit a record high,"
by Charlotte Edmond, World Economic Forum, June 20, 2017.

"If they do have to migrate then they want to be supported to migrate with dignity. Or to migrate in ways that support their futures."

She says that whilst climate migration is a last resort, it should be done in a way that supports livelihoods and social networks, and works to minimise physical and mental health impacts.

Like other Small Island Developing States in the Pacific Region, Fiji faces financial challenges responding to climate disasters. As a result, climate finance is a high priority for discussion at COP23 for Fijian Prime Minister and incoming COP23 President Frank Bainimarama.

The Fijian government recently hosted a COP23 delegation for some pre-COP 'Partnership Day,' where he described the plight of his people.

"It matters that you have come to Fiji, to where we live, to see the impact that climate change is having on our way of life," he said. "And to perhaps understand better the specific vulnerability of people living in Small Island Developing States."

He also gave a summary of Fiji's vision for COP23, and articulated the importance of action and progress.

"Fiji's vision is for a Presidency that is transparent and inclusive of all, advances the Paris Agreement and accelerates climate action for all vulnerable societies, drawing on our own experiences as a Small Island Developing State in the Pacific.

"We are all vulnerable and we all need to act."

A Four-Degree Rise in Global Temperatures Could Trigger a Worldwide Economic Depression

Tom Kompas

In the following viewpoint Tom Kompas argues that the impending crisis of climate change could potentially cause a worldwide depression similar to the Great Depression of the United States in the 1930s. The author contends that this crisis could happen with as little as a four-degree change in global temperatures, and it will occur if governments and people don't seriously address issues like greenhouse gas emissions and consider the behavior of producers and consumers in creating possible climate models. Kompas is a Professor of Environmental Economics and Biosecurity in the School of Biosciences and the School of Ecosystem and Forest Sciences at the University of Melbourne.

As you read, consider the following questions:

1. In what ways might the world experience a global version of the Great Depression?
2. What were some of the results of applying a new dimensional global trade model?
3. What seems to be the relationship between countries that emit the most greenhouse gas emissions and the impact of climate change so far?

"U.S. $23 trillion will be lost if temperatures rise four degrees by 2100," by Tom Kompas, Phys.org, August 15, 2018.

E conomic modelling suggests this is the reality facing us if we continue emitting greenhouse gases and allowing temperatures to rise unabated.

Economists have largely underestimated the global economic damages from climate change, partly as a result of averaging these effects across countries and regions, but also because the likely behavior of producers and consumers in a climate change future isn't usually taken into consideration in climate modelling.

Model Is Conservative

The sleepy lizard awakens new tools for climate change research. In a recent work published in Earth's Future, an open access journal of the American Geophysical Union, colleagues at the University of Melbourne, Australia National University, CSIRO and I developed a large dimensional global trade model to better account for various effects of global warming on national incomes for 139 countries.

This is the first large dimensional model that captures damages for each country from climate change, allowing for a measure of extremes, without averaging, along with forward-looking behavior.

It is a conservative model, in that it only accounts for some of the impacts of climate change—loss in agricultural productivity, sea level changes, human health and productivity effects. It doesn't account for losses from extreme weather events or the increased frequency of fire damage.

The good news is that our model shows considerable global economic gains from complying with the Paris Climate Accord, which sets a goal of limiting global temperature increases this century to below 2 degrees Celsius.

However, based on current emissions, climate models range in their predictions from a 3.2 degrees Celsius increase in global temperatures to a 5.9 degrees Celsius increase. A recent study published in *Nature* indicates a 93 per cent chance that temperatures will exceed 4 degrees Celsius of warming with 'business at usual.'

Severe Consequences

We examine both the 4 degrees Celsius and 3 degrees Celsius scenarios, compared to the 2 degrees Celsius case.

The estimated damages from not complying with the Paris Accord are severe. At 4 degrees Celsius of global warming, for example, the losses in income to the global economy are over US$23 trillion per year, or the equivalent in economic damage of three or four 2008 Global Financial Crises each year.

These damages represent roughly one-third of current global GDP and about 7 per cent or more of projected GDP in 2100.

At 3 degrees Celsius, the losses are over US$9.5 trillion.

Our work underscores the benefits of complying with the Paris Climate Accord. For example, relative to a temperature increase of 4 degrees Celsius, the global gains from complying with the 2-degree target are over US$17 trillion per year in the long run, while the global gains at keeping global temperature rises to 3 degrees Celsius are still nearly US$4 trillion per year.

Poorer Countries Worse Hit

It is often stated that poorer countries are the ones most impacted by climate change, and our model underscores this point. Countries in South Asia, Southeast Asia and Africa are severely impacted at all temperature increases. The losses in GDP are dramatic.

Losses, for example, at 4 degrees Celsius, for Cambodia, Sri Lanka, and Nicaragua are over 17 per cent, for Indonesia 19 per cent, for India 14 per cent, Thailand 17 per cent, Singapore 16 per cent, and the Philippines 20 per cent. For much of Africa the losses range from 18 to over 26 per cent of GDP.

These results emphasize the equity problem that goes with these effects—many countries that are major per capita greenhouse gas emitters are the ones less impacted by climate change.

Global losses of this size are comparable to the Great Depression of the 1930s, with its global fall in GDP of 15 per cent, except these will occur year after year, with no way for effective redress.

This raises another concern. The severe falls in GDP in the long term will put many governments under fiscal stress, since tax revenues are tied to GDP or national income levels. Tax revenues will fall dramatically.

In addition, if global warming is linked to increases in the frequency of weather events and other natural disasters, which invoke significant emergency management responses and expenditures, the pressure on government budgets will be even more severe.

Severe Weather to Make Matters Worse

Many governments around the globe won't be able to cope and will, to put it simply, fail.

It's worth noting that damages in this modelling for Australia are relatively mild compared to much of the rest of the world, but even here they are significant.

Without significant weather effects included in the modelling, and at 4 degrees Celsius global warming, damages per person in Australia are projected to be US$4,886, or roughly US$13,945 per household, per year, every year.

We are now extending this work to account for increases in the frequency and severity of weather events induced by climate change. Early results for the effects of tropical storms alone indicate that global economic damages increase significantly, at all temperature ranges, and more than double the more than US$23 trillion in global economic damages at 4 degrees Celsius found in the current paper.

Specific Patterns of Climate Changes Have Closely Matched the Predicted Effects of Greenhouse Gas Emissions

Spencer Weart

In the following excerpted viewpoint, Spencer Weart presents a historical view of changes in climate, temperature, and other indicators since the 1930s. As scientists began closely monitoring changes in climate and trends toward both cooling and warming, they began to realize that their data was indicating a serious change in the climate system. And yet, despite this continuously accumulating data, people continue to argue about whether climate change is a trend or a serious and rapidly worsening situation. Weart was the former director of the Center for History of Physics of the American Institute of Physics from 1971–2009.

As you read, consider the following questions:

1. What were some of the "hints of warming" in the era of 1930–1950?
2. Why did some scientists feel that global temperatures were cooling in the 1960s and 1970s?
3. What were the results of the 1977 US Department of Defense survey?

"The Modern Temperature Trend," by Spencer Weart, American Institute of Physics, February 2018. https://history.aip.org/climate/20ctrend.htm. Reprinted by permission.

Tracking the world's average temperature from the late 19th century, people in the 1930s realized there had been a pronounced warming trend. During the 1960s, weather experts found that over the past couple of decades the trend had shifted to cooling. With a new awareness that climate could change in serious ways, in the early 1970s some scientists predicted a continued gradual cooling, perhaps a phase of a long natural cycle or perhaps caused by human pollution of the atmosphere with smog and dust. Others insisted that the effects of such pollution were temporary, and humanity's emission of greenhouse gases would bring warming over the long run. All of them agreed that their knowledge was primitive and any prediction was guesswork. But understanding of the climate system was advancing swiftly. The view that warming must dominate won out in the late 1970s as it became clear that the cooling spell (mainly a Northern Hemisphere effect) had indeed been a temporary distraction. When the rise continued into the 21st century, penetrating even into the ocean depths, scientists recognized that it signaled a profound change in the climate system. Nothing like it had been seen for centuries, and probably not for millennia. The specific pattern of changes, revealed in objects ranging from ship logs to ice caps to tree rings, closely matched the predicted effects of greenhouse gas emissions.

If you had a certain type of mind, temperature statistics could be more absorbing than a book of crossword puzzles. Ever since the invention of the thermometer, some amateur and professional scientists had recorded the temperature wherever they happened to be living or visiting. Government weather services began to record measurements more systematically during the 19th century. By the 1930s, observers had accumulated millions of numbers for temperatures at stations around the world. It was an endlessly challenging task to weed out the unreliable data, average the rest in clever combinations, and compare the results for each particular region with other weather features such as droughts. Many of the players in this game pursued a hope of discovering cycles of weather that could lead to predictions. Perhaps, for example, one could correlate rainfall trends with the eleven-year sunspot cycle.

Hints of Warming (1930s–1950s)

Adding interest to the game was a suspicion that temperatures had generally increased since the late 19th century—at least in eastern North America and western Europe, the only parts of the world where reliable measurements went back so far.[2] In the 1930s, the press began to call attention to numerous anecdotes of above-normal temperatures. The head of the US Weather Bureau's Division of Climate and Crop Weather responded in 1934. "With 'Grand-Dad' insisting that the winters were colder and the snows deeper when he was a lad," he said, "... it was decided to make a rather exhaustive study of the question." Averaging results from many stations in the eastern United States and some scattered locations elsewhere around the world, the weather services found that "Grand-Dad" was right: since 1865 average temperatures had risen several degrees Fahrenheit (°F) in most regions. Experts thought this was simply one phase of a cycle of rising and falling temperatures that probably ambled along for centuries. As one scientist explained, when he spoke of the current "climate change" he did not mean any permanent shift, but a long-term cyclical change "like all other climate fluctuations."[3]

It may have been the press reports of warming that stimulated an English engineer, Guy Stewart Callendar, to take up climate study as an amateur enthusiast. He undertook a thorough and systematic effort to look for historical changes in the average temperature of the entire planet. One 19th-century German had already made an attempt at this, seeking a connection with sunspot cycles. Otherwise, if anyone else had thought about it, they had probably been discouraged by the scattered and irregular character of the weather records, plus the common assumption that the average climate scarcely changed over the span of a century. But since the late 19th century meteorologists around the world had been meticulously compiling weather records, and had spent countless hours negotiating standards so the data from different countries and different years could be compared on the same basis. Callendar drew upon that massive international effort. After countless hours of sorting out data and penciling sums, he announced that the mean global temperature had definitely risen between 1890 and 1935, by close to half a degree Celsius (0.5°C, equal to 0.9°F).[4]

Callendar's statistics gave him confidence to push ahead with another and more audacious claim. Reviving an old theory that human emissions of carbon dioxide gas (CO_2) from burning fuel could cause a "greenhouse effect," Callendar said this was the cause of the warming.

It all sounded dubious to most meteorologists. Temperature data were such a mess of random fluctuations that with enough manipulation you could derive all sorts of spurious trends. Taking a broader look, experts believed that climate was comfortably uniform. "There is no scientific reason to believe that our climate will change radically in the next few decades," the highly respected climatologist Helmut Landsberg explained in 1946. "Good and poor years will occur with approximately the same frequency as heretofore."[5] If during some decades in some region there was an unmistakable climate change, the change must be just part of some local cycle, and in due time the climate of the region would revert to its average.

(By the end of the 20th century, scientists were able to check Callendar's figures. They had done far more extensive and sophisticated analysis of the weather records, confirmed by "proxy" data such as studies of tree rings and measurements of old temperatures that lingered in deep boreholes. The data showed that the world had in fact been warming from the mid 19th century up to about 1940. As it happened, much of the warming had been in the relatively small patch of the planet that contained the United States and Europe—and thus contained the great majority of scientists and weather records. If not for this accident, people might have paid little attention to the idea of global warming for another generation. That would have severely delayed our understanding of what we face.)

During the 1940s only a few people looked into the question of warming. A prominent example was the Swedish scientist Hans Ahlmann, who voiced concern about the strong warming seen in some northern regions since early in the century. But in 1952, he reported that northern temperatures had begun to fall again since around 1940.[6] The argument for warming caused by CO_2 emissions, another eminent climatologist wrote in 1949, "has rather broken down in the last few years" when temperatures in some regions fell. However, scarcely a year later he allowed that since 1850 glaciers had been in retreat, and noted that "Winter temperatures rose over a large part of the northern hemisphere."[7] In any case (as yet another authority remarked), compared with the vast slow swings of ice ages, "the recent oscillations of climate have been relatively small."[8]

If the North Atlantic region was no longer warming, through the 1940s and 1950s it remained balmy in comparison with earlier decades. People were beginning to doubt the assumption of climate stability. Several scientists published analyses of weather records that confirmed Callendar's finding of an overall rise since the 1880s.[9] An example was a careful study of US Weather Bureau data by Landsberg, who was now the Bureau's chief climatologist. The results persuaded him to abandon his belief that the climate was unchanging. He found an undeniable and significant warming in the first half of the century, especially in more northern latitudes. He thought it might be due either to variations in the Sun's energy or to the rise of CO_2.[10] Others pitched in with reports of effects plain enough to persuade attentive members of the public. Ahlmann for one announced that glaciers were retreating, crops were growing farther north, and the like.[11] Another striking example was a report that in the Arctic "the ice is thinner at the present than ever before in historic times;" before long we might even see an open polar sea.[12] Such high-latitude effects were exactly what simple models suggested would result from the greenhouse effect warming of increased CO2.

"Our attitude to climatic 'normals' must clearly change," wrote the respected climate historian Hubert H. Lamb in 1959. Recent decades could not be called normal by any standard of the past, and he saw no reason to expect the next decades would be "normal" either. Actually, since the 1930s the temperatures in his own homeland, Britain, had been heading down, but Lamb would not speculate whether that was the start of a cyclical downtrend. It could be "merely another wobble" in one region. Lamb's main point, reinforced by his scholarly studies of weather reports clear back to medieval times, was that regional climate change could be serious and long-lasting.[14] Most meteorologists nevertheless stuck to their belief that the only changes to be expected were moderate swings in one part of the world or another, with a fairly prompt return to the long-term average. If there was almost a consensus that for the time being there was a world-wide tendency to warming, the agreement was fragile.

Warming or Cooling? (1960s–1974)

In January 1961, on a snowy and unusually cold day in New York City, J. Murray Mitchell, Jr. of the US Weather Bureau's Office of Climatology told a meeting of meteorologists that the world's temperature was falling. Independently of Callendar (who had meanwhile been updating and improving his own global temperature history), Mitchell had trudged through all the exacting calculations, working out average temperatures for most of the globe, and got plausible results. He confirmed that global temperatures had risen until about 1940. But since then, he reported, temperatures had been falling. There was so much random variation from place to place and from year to year that the reversal to cooling had only now become unambiguous.[14*]

Acknowledging that the increasing amount of CO2 in the atmosphere should give a tendency for warming, Mitchell tentatively suggested that smoke from recent volcanic eruptions and perhaps cyclical changes in the Sun might partly account for the reversal. (Later studies confirmed that volcanoes, and possibly a decline in solar activity, probably did have some cooling effect around that time.) But he rightly held that "such theories appear to be insufficient to account for the recent cooling," and he could only conclude that the downturn was "a curious enigma." He suspected the cooling might be part of a natural "rhythm," a cycle lasting 80 years or so.[15] The veteran science correspondent Walter Sullivan was at the meeting, and he reported in the *New York Times* (January 25 and 30, 1961) that after days of discussion the meteorologists generally agreed on the existence of the cooling trend, but could not agree on a cause for this or any other climate change. "Many schools of thought were represented ... and, while the debate remained good-humored, there was energetic dueling with scientific facts." The confused state of climate science was a public embarrassment.

Through the 1960s and into the 1970s, the average global temperature remained relatively cool. Western Europe in particular suffered some of the coldest winters on record. (Studies in later decades found that a quasi-regular long-term weather cycle in the North Atlantic Ocean had moved into a phase in the 1960s that encouraged Arctic winds to move southward there.)[16] People (including scientists) will always give special attention to the weather that they see when they walk out their doors, and what they saw made them doubt that global warming was at hand. In the early 1970s, wherever climate experts got together they debated whether the world was due to get warmer or cooler. Callendar found the turn worrisome, and contacted climate experts to discuss it.[17] Landsberg returned to his earlier view that the climate was probably showing only transient fluctuations, not a rising trend. While pollution and CO2 might be altering the climate in limited regions, he wrote, "on the global scale natural forces still prevail." He added, however, that "this should not lead to complacency" about the risk of global changes in the distant future.[18]

One source of confusion was increasingly debated. Weather watchers had long recognized that the central parts of cities were distinctly warmer than the surrounding countryside. In urban areas the absorption of solar energy by smog, black roads and roofs, along with direct outpouring of heat from furnaces and other energy sources, created an "urban heat island" effect. This was the most striking of all human modifications of local climates. It could be snowing in the suburbs while raining downtown.[19] Some people pushed ahead to suggest that as human civilization used ever more energy, in a century or so the direct output of heat could be great enough to disturb the entire global climate.[20] If so, that would not happen soon, and for the moment the main consequences were statistical.

Some experts began to ask whether the warming reported for the decades before 1940 had been an illusion. Most temperature measurements came from built-up areas. As the cities grew, so did their local heating, which might have given a spurious impression of global warming.[21*] Callendar and others replied that they were well aware of urban effects, and took them fully into account in their calculations. Mitchell in particular agreed that population growth could explain the "record high" temperatures often reported in American cities—but it could not explain the warming of remote Arctic regions.[22*] Yet the statistical difficulties were so complex that the global warming up to 1940 remained in doubt. Some skeptics continued to argue that the warming was a mere illusion caused by urbanization.

While neither scientists nor the public could be sure in the 1970s whether the world was warming or cooling, people were increasingly inclined to believe that global climate was on the move, and in no small way. The reassuring assumption of a stable "normal" climate was rarely heard now. In the early 1970s, a series of ruinous droughts and other exceptionally bad spells of weather in various parts of the world provoked warnings that world food stocks might run out. Fears increased that somehow humanity was at fault for the bad weather—if we were not causing global warming with greenhouse gases, then perhaps we were cooling the globe with our smoke and smog. Responding to public anxieties, in 1973 the Japan Meteorological Agency sent a questionnaire to meteorological services around the world. They found no consensus. Most agencies reported that they saw no clear climate trend, but several (including the Japanese themselves) noted a recent cooling in many regions. Many experts thought it likely that the world had entered a long-term cool spell.[23]

Public pressure was urging scientists to declare where the climate was going. But they could not do so without knowing what caused climate changes. Haze in the air from volcanoes might explain some cooling, but not as much as was observed. A few experts worried that pollution from human sources, such as dust from overgrazed lands and haze from factories, was beginning to shade and cool the planet's surface. But most experts doubted we were putting out enough air pollution to seriously affect global climate. A more acceptable explanation was a traditional one: the Earth was responding to long-term fluctuations in the Sun's output of energy.[24]

An alternative explanation was found in the "Milankovitch" cycles, tens of thousands of years long, that astronomers calculated for minor variations in the Earth's orbit. These variations brought cyclical changes in the amount of sunlight reaching a given latitude on Earth. In 1966, a leading climate expert analyzed the cycles and predicted that we were starting on the descent into a new ice age.[25] In the early 1970s, a variety of measurements pinned down the nature and timing of the cycles as actually reflected in past climate shifts. Projecting the cycles forward strengthened the prediction. A gradual cooling seemed to be astronomically scheduled over the next few thousand years. Later and better calculations would make that tens of thousands of years, but at the time a few people speculated that we might even see substantial natural cooling within centuries.[26] Unless, that is, something intervened.

Warming Resumed (1975–1987)

It scarcely mattered what the Milankovitch orbital changes might do, wrote Murray Mitchell in 1972, since "man's intervention ... would if anything tend to prolong the present interglacial." Human industry would prevent an advance of the ice by blanketing the Earth with CO2. A panel of top experts convened by the National Academy of Sciences in 1975 tentatively agreed with Mitchell. True, in recent years the temperature had been dropping (perhaps as part of some unknown "longer-period climatic oscillation"). And industrial haze might also have a cooling effect, perhaps reinforcing the natural long-term trend toward a new ice age. Nevertheless, they thought CO2 "could conceivably" bring half a degree of warming by the end of the century.[27] The outspoken geochemist and oceanographer Wallace Broecker went farther. He suspected that there was indeed a natural cycle responsible for the cooling in recent decades, perhaps originating in cyclical changes on the Sun. If so, it was only temporarily canceling the greenhouse warming. Within a few decades that would climb past any natural cycle. Although it turned out he was wrong about the natural cycle, this was one of several occasions when Broecker's scientific instincts about general processes were better than his specific calculations. Introducing a new phrase, he asked, "Are we on the brink of a pronounced global warming?"[28*]

[…]

The tendency of some scientists in the early 1970s to suspect that the world was cooling now collapsed. Science journalists reported that climate scientists were openly divided, and those who expected warming were increasingly numerous. A good example is Hubert Lamb, the historian of climate who in the 1950s had called attention to climate changes without attempting to predict them. Generalizing from the unusually good historical records in his native England, Lamb had depicted a globally warm "Medieval Climatic Optimum" followed in the early modern period by a "Little Ice Age." During the chilly 1960s he was persuaded by the studies of natural cycles that a new ice age was likely to arrive over thousands of years. But after the hot English summer of 1976 he joined the emerging viewpoint that human greenhouse gas emissions would "become dominant over the natural climate fluctuations by about A.D. 2000."[31]

In an attempt to force scientists to agree on a useful answer, in 1977 the US Department of Defense persuaded two dozen of the world's top climate experts to respond to a complicated survey. Their main conclusion was that scientific knowledge was meager and all predictions were unreliable. The panel was nearly equally divided among three opinions: some thought further cooling was likely, others suspected that moderate greenhouse warming would begin fairly soon, and most of the rest expected the climate would stay about the same at least for the next couple of decades. Only a few thought it probable that there would be considerable global warming by the year 2000.[31a]

Government officials and scientists wanted more definite statements on what was happening to the weather. Thousands of stations around the world were turning out daily numbers, but these represented many different standards and degrees of reliability—a disorderly, almost indigestible mess. Just storing the records was a formidable challenge. Already in 1966, "From storage rooms to hallways, punch card file cabinets containing the nation's archive of climate data filled every conceivable space at the National Weather Records Center (NWRC) ... There was concern that the NWRC building was in imminent danger of a structural collapse." Although computer memory storage technology improved with tremendous speed, the ever-increasing volume of data kept pace.[31b]

[...]

Notes

2. One early notice was Brooks (1922).
3. Kincer (1934), p. 62; "wie bei allen anderen Klimaschwankugen": Scherhag (1937), p. 263; similarly, "no evidence" of a permanent shift: George E. McEwen of Scripps, Science Newsletter (1940).

4. Callendar (1938). Early attempt: Köppen (1873). On the "World Weather Records" see Le Treut et al. (2007), pp. 101–102.

5. Landsberg (1946), pp. 297–98.

6. Abarbanel and McCluskey (1950), p. 23, see *New York Times*, May 30, 1947 and August 7, 1952.

7. Brooks (1949), p. 117; Brooks (March 1950), p. 113.

8. Willett (1949), p. 50.

9. In particular, Lysgaard (1950); this was cited by several authors in Shapley (1953); see also Willett (1950); on the shift of views, see Lamb (1966b), 171–72, also ix, 1–2.

10. Landsberg (1958); his analysis found an average 0.8°F rise, more around the Great Lakes. Landsberg (1960).

11. Ahlmann (1952).

12. Crary et al. (1955).

13. Lamb (1959), in Changing Climate (1966) p. 19.

14. Mitchell was spurred by some Scandinavian studies showing a leveling off in the 1950s—the Arctic was usually where trends showed up first. Mitchell (1961); see also Mitchell (1963), "rhythm" p. 180. In his independent calculation, Callendar (1961) found chiefly a temperature rise in the Arctic. For another and similar temperature curve, computed by the Main Geophysical Observatory in Leningrad (and attributed to volcanoes), see Budyko (1969), p. 612. An expert called the works of Mitchell, Callendar (1961), and Budyko "the first reasonably reliable estimates of large scale average temperatures," Wigley et al. (1986), p. 278. One other attempt was Willett (1950).

15. Mitchell (1961), pp. 249, 247.

16. For the North Atlantic Oscillation, see Fagan (2000), esp. pp. 207–08.

17. At a 1972 meeting in Stockholm, for example, there was an impasse between "the climate 'coolers' and the climate 'warmers,'" Kellogg (1987), pp. 122–23. Callendar: Lamb (1997), p. 218.

18. Landsberg (1967); quote: Landsberg (1970), p. 1273; on all this, see Mitchell (1991).

19. Brief reviews of observations back to the 19th century include Mitchell (1953); Landsberg (1955); Landsberg (1970).

20. Budyko (1962); others such as Wilson and Matthews (1971) pp. 60, 166–68 agreed the effect could be serious.

21. e.g., Dronia (1967), removing urban heat effects found no net warming since the 19th century.

22. Mitchell (1953); already in 1938 Callendar adjusted for the effect, while admitting that "this is a matter which is open to controversy." Callendar (1938), p. 235. Additionally, the common practice during the 1950s of moving weather stations from downtown locations to airports, outside the "heat island," would give a spurious impression of cooling, but Mitchell and others allowed for that too in their calculations.

23. Lamb (1977), pp. 709–10.

24. Johnsen et al. (1970); Lamb (1977), pp. 529, 549.

25. Emiliani (1966b).

26. Hays et al. (1976).

27. Mitchell (1972), p. 445; GARP (1975), pp. 37, 43; they cite a Manabe computer model of 1971 and Mitchell (1973).

28. Broecker (1975). The only known earlier use of "global warming" was in a small-town newspaper, *The Hammond Times* (Indiana), November 6, 1957. See Ari Jokimäki, "Was Broecker really the first to use the term Global Warming?" skepticalscience.com, September 30, 2015, online here.

31. Lamb (1977), p. 698n1, citing a 1976 World Meteorological Organization statement (noted here).

31a. National Defense University (1978); also published in Council on Environmental Quality (1980), ch. 17.

31b. Edwards (2010); quote: Steurer (2007).

Periodical and Internet Sources Bibliography

The following articles have been selected to supplement the diverse views presented in this chapter.

Susana B. Adamo, "Migration, Displacement and Climate Change." Columbia University, April 25, 2016. http://www.un.org/en/ development/desa/population/migration/events/other/other/ documents/250416_COLUMBIA_UNI_Susana_Adamo.pdf

Laignee Barron, "143 Million People Could Soon Be Displaced Because of Climate Change, World Bank Says." *TIME*, March 20, 2018. http://time.com/5206716/world-bank-climate-change-internal-migration/

Hildegard Bedarff, "Climate Change, Migration, and Displacement: The Underestimated Disaster." Greenpeace Germany, 2017. https://www.greenpeace.de/sites/www.greenpeace.de/ files/20170524-greenpeace-studie-climate-change-migration-displacement-engl.pdf

"Climate Displacement in Bangladesh." Environmental Justice Foundation, 2017. https://ejfoundation.org/reports/climate-displacement-in-bangladesh

Cornell University, "Rising seas could result in 2 billion refugees by 2100." Science News, June 26, 2017. https://www.sciencedaily. com/releases/2017/06/170626105746.htm

Catherine Devitt, "Climate Change and Population Displacement." Working Notes, April 26, 2016. https://www.workingnotes.ie/ poverty2/item/climate-change-and-population-displacement

Jeff Goodell, "Welcome to the Age of Climate Migration." *Rolling Stone*, February 25, 2018. https://www.rollingstone.com/politics/ politics-news/welcome-to-the-age-of-climate-migration-202221/

Intergovernmental Panel on Climate Change, "Climate Extremes and Migration." Intergovernmental Panel on Climate Change (IPCC), 2018. http://www.ipcc.ch/ipccreports/tar/wg2/index. php?idp=450

Walter Kälin, "Displacement Caused by the Effects of Climate Change: Who Will Be Affected and What Are the Gaps in the Normative Framework for Their Protection?" Brookings Institute, October 10, 2008. https://www.brookings.edu/research/displacement-caused-by-the-effects-of-climate-change-who-will-be-affected-and-what-are-the-gaps-in-the-normative-framework-for-their-protection/

Baher Kamal, "Climate Migrants Might Reach One Billion by 2050." Reliefweb, August 21, 2017. https://reliefweb.int/report/world/climate-migrants-might-reach-one-billion-2050

Kevin Krajick, "Climate Migrants Will Soon Shift Populations of Many Countries, Says World Bank." State of the Planet, Columbia University, March 19, 2018. https://blogs.ei.columbia.edu/2018/03/19/climate-refugees-will/

GLOBALVIEWPOINTS

CHAPTER 2

The Causes and Effects of Climate Change Migration

Some Regions May Be Uninhabitable by the End of the Century

David Funkhouser

In the following viewpoint David Funkhouser presents evidence that climate change will transform some areas of the world into places that are uninhabitable by humans, due to hotter temperatures, flooding, droughts, and other events that make it impossible for humans to survive. In addition, because the consequences of climate change are affecting poorer, undeveloped countries the most, it is the responsibility of developed countries to address the causes. Funkouser is a writer and former content manager and science writer for the Earth Institute and the Lamont-Doherty Earth Observatory at Columbia University.

As you read, consider the following questions:

1. What were the two conclusions that Hansen and Sato reached as a result of their research?
2. What did the study note about shifts in US temperature between summer and winter?
3. What do the authors feel is the only solution to reducing carbon emissions?

"Climate May Make Some Regions 'Uninhabitable' by End of Century," by David Funkhouser, Earth Institute Columbia University, March 2, 2016. Reprinted by permission.

The global trend toward hotter summers could make parts of the Middle East and tropics "practically uninhabitable" by the end of the century, new research published this week contends.

The work, by climate scientist James Hansen and Makiko Sato of Columbia University's Program on Climate Science, Awareness and Solutions, builds on earlier research showing that summers generally are more often becoming hotter than the average recorded between 1951–1980. The new paper updates their analysis of the data and looks at how temperatures are changing region by region. The authors conclude that summers in particular have continued to grow hotter, and that extreme heat events are occurring more frequently.

They warn that the increased heat intensifies drought in the subtropics, and combined with other effects of climate change such as sea level rise, increased floods and impacts on human health, could be devastating. And they argue that a tax or fee on carbon is the only way to quickly address the threats from climate change.

"The overall message that climate science delivers to society, policymakers and the public alike is this: We have a global emergency," writes Hansen in an accompanying summary of the paper.

Hansen has in the past referred to the temperature shifts as "loading the climate dice." Because of the natural variability of climate, some summers are colder and some hotter than others. Plotted on a graph over time, these fall into a bell curve on which most summers fall somewhere in the middle. Imagine six-sided dice: two sides are "normal," two are "hot" and two are "cold."

Now, shift the graph toward hotter: Now the "average" summer is hotter than before. On your dice, perhaps three sides are "hot" and just one "cold"—raising the odds that summer will be hotter than what used to be considered "normal." This is what is happening around the world, in varying degrees.

"Global warming of about 1°F (0.6°C) over the past several decades now 'loads the climate dice,'" Hansen said. "We showed earlier that the 'bell curve' of seasonal mean temperature anomalies

Could Climate Change Cause Mass Human Migration?

The world has witnessed some of the greatest scenes of mass migration in recent years, after the crisis in Syria forced millions of civilians to flee to Europe. As devastating as these scenes are, they are likely to be just a saddening taste of the displacement that could be caused by the threat from climate change.

The so-called "climate change refugees" are expected to number between 250 and 1,000 million people over the next 50 years, according to estimates by the United Nations High Commissioner for Refugees (UNHCR).

Last year, the Intergovernmental Panel on Climate Change (IPCC) explicitly recognized that "climate change over the 21st century is projected to increase the displacement of people." Furthermore, it "can indirectly increase risks of violent conflicts in the form of civil war and inter-group violence by amplifying well-documented drivers of these conflicts such as poverty and economic shocks."

Although these are only projected numbers, "there are already people who are being forced from their homes by climate change. For example, in the Arctic, which is warming at twice the rate of the planet, indigenous communities are being forced to relocate inland because their villages are literally falling into the sea," said Alice Thomas, climate displacement program manager at Refugees International.

This forced displacement, which is a result of natural disasters, has been a major problem worldwide. Since 2008, an average of 22.5 million people have relocated each year from their homes, following weather-related disasters brought on by floods, storms, wildfires and extreme temperatures. It is expected that this situation will be exacerbated in the coming years due to the effects of global warming.

Climate change causes an increase in the frequency and force of extreme weather such as mega-floods, super-typhoons and prolonged drought. It's why extreme weather events may become the norm, rather than the exception.

"Could climate change cause mass human migration?" by Daniel Casillas, Metro Media US, March 18, 2016.

has shifted so far that people can notice that extreme hot summers now occur more often than they did 50 years ago. However, we show here that there are strong regional variations in this bell curve shift, and that the largest effects occur in nations least responsible for causing climate change."

The paper, "Regional climate change and national responsibilities," was published Wednesday in Environmental Research Letters. The authors present data showing variations in how much hotter things have gotten in different regions of the world.

The shift in summer temperatures in the United States is greater than the warming in winter. As a result, people are likely to notice summers getting warmer, but not necessarily winters.

According to Hansen, summers cooler than the average 1951–1980 summer still occur, but only about 19 percent of the time. Extreme summer heat, defined as 3 standard deviations or more warmer than the 1951–1980 average, which almost never occurred 50 years ago, now occur with a frequency of about 7 percent.

By contrast, Hansen notes, in the Mediterranean and Middle East, "every summer is now warmer than the average 1951–1980 climate, and the period with 'summer' climate is now considerably longer." The changes are "far exceeding natural variability" in the climate, he said.

"Given that summers were already very hot in this region, the change affects livability and productivity," Hansen writes. "The tropics and the Middle East in summer are in danger of becoming practically uninhabitable by the end of the century if business-as-usual fossil fuel emissions continue, because wet bulb temperature could approach the level at which the human body is unable to cool itself under even well-ventilated outdoor conditions," he writes.

"Lesser warming still makes life more difficult and reduces productivity in these regions, because temperatures are approaching the limit of human tolerance, and both agricultural and construction work are mainly outdoor activities."

Europe is showing more warming than in the United States. And in China, the warming trend should be noticeable in both summer and winter to people old enough to recall the seasons of 50 years ago, the researchers said. In India, the shift is even larger.

Hansen notes that "increasing temperature seems to have a significant effect on violence and human conflict, as indicated by a body of empirical evidence in a rapidly expanding area of scientific study." That would include a 2015 study co-authored by Earth Institute scientists that concluded that the drought in Syria influenced the outbreak of the civil war there. Hansen cites other studies that have correlated increases in violence with increases in temperature.

The paper also updates an analysis of how different countries have contributed to climate change, primarily through burning fossil fuels and emitting carbon dioxide and other gases that contribute to the warming. While China has taken the lead in overall emissions today, historically the United States and Europe each are responsible for more than a quarter of the climate change we see today, the paper contends.

The authors argue that the developed countries bear a greater responsibility to address the issue. It also argues that the historic climate agreement reached in Paris in December, in which the world's nations agreed on goals for reducing emissions, won't fix the problem.

"We argue that country-by-country goals, the approach of the 21st Conference of the Parties [in Paris] cannot lead to rapid phase-down of fossil fuel emissions, as long as fossil fuels are allowed to be the cheapest energy," the authors say. The only solution, they add, is to start imposing a fee on carbon that recognizes the negative impact that burning up fossil fuels has had on the environment.

In Bangladesh, Chad, and the United States Mass Climate Migration Is a Growing Global Crisis

Marcus Arcanjo

In the following viewpoint Marcus Arcanjo shows that climate migration is already taking place across wide areas of the world, and the numbers of refugees are increasing. He focuses on three countries: Bangladesh, Chad, and the United States, and how climate migration is affecting them. Bangladesh is being threatened by rising sea levels and overpopulation, Chad is suffering from ongoing regional conflicts and prolonged droughts, and the US is experiencing regular hurricanes and heat waves. Each country will have different issues to deal with, issues that affect the rests of the world as well. Arcanjo is a Research Fellow at the Climate Institute.

As you read, consider the following questions:

1. Why are Bangladesh, Chad, and the United States all experiencing climate migration? Do they have factors in common?
2. What factors make Bangladesh at risk from climate change and likely to experience climate migration?
3. In addition to climate change, what other factors put Chad at risk for migration?

"Climate Migration: A Growing Global Crisis," by Marcus Arcanjo, Climate Institute, April 30, 2018. Reprinted by permission.

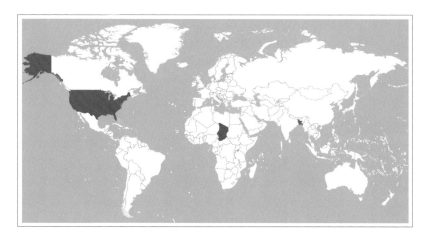

Climate migration is increasing and widespread. Although much of the literature on this topic focuses on island states, these territories represent a comparatively small fraction of a much greater problem. According to the World Bank, migration is expected to soar by 2050 unless carbon emissions are rapidly curbed. As average temperatures increase, causing coastal flooding and prolonged droughts, upwards of 140 million people globally are likely to become displaced. Worryingly, even if average temperatures fall below the ambitious 2-degree Celsius target set out in the Paris Agreement, 40 million people will remain vulnerable. Worst-case scenarios provide a pessimistic glimpse into the future, with an anticipated displacement of 85 million people in Sub-Saharan Africa alone. These are some of the poorest people in the world, and many lack the necessary resources to relocate. As a consequence, they face the very real possibility of being trapped in places that are rapidly becoming uninhabitable.

This paper explores climate migration in three countries: Bangladesh, Chad, and the United States. Each nation has different climate vulnerabilities and enormously varied capacities to adapt, yet all are experiencing mass migration that will likely continue far into the future. Bangladesh is being threatened by rising sea levels and the overpopulation of its capital, while Chad is suffering from ongoing regional conflicts exacerbated by prolonged droughts. The

US, for its part, is experiencing regular hurricanes and heat waves that have forced people to abandon their homes. After analyzing these disparate case studies, this paper will address the important debate surrounding refugee status—suggesting, in turn, that the current status raises a moral issue given that climate migrants are not afforded the same rights as those currently classified as refugees. In this vein, and in order to provide better protection for those fleeing ecological degradation and climate change, this paper suggests that a rethink of refugee status so as to encompass climate and environmental issues may be required.

Bangladesh: A Drowning Nation

Bangladesh has had a tough time of it when it comes to climate change. It is one of the states most vulnerable to this phenomenon, and faces great uncertainty. Its capital, Dhaka, has a population of 18 million, which is rapidly rising. In 2015, it was estimated that 2,000 migrants a day moved to the city. Critically, 70 percent of these were escaping environmental degradation. The country lies just one meter above sea level, placing its citizens in an enormously precarious position. Regular flooding caused by heavy monsoon rains, coupled with temperature increases and ensuing rises in sea level, have led scientists to predict that up to 25 percent of Bangladesh's total landmass will be lost over the coming decades. The national government's strategy paper on this topic anticipates that loss of land to result in 25 million climate refugees; independent estimates are even higher. The country does not have the capacity to support such widespread devastation and displacement. A full 50 million of its inhabitants already live in poverty, with a large proportion of these based in ecologically fragile areas.

Compounding those problems is the fact that glacial melt from the Himalayas regularly causes walls of water to flood the Bay of Bengal. This low-lying region is particularly vulnerable as a result. With the worsening climate, it has also suffered from increasingly frequent storms and cyclones. Indeed, 60 percent of global deaths from cyclones over the last two decades occurred in Bangladesh.

Cyclone Aila (2009) alone left a million people homeless, and permanently ruined precious farmland for thousands more. The salinization resulting from such a disaster pollutes drinking supplies and renders agriculture almost impossible. The International Organisation for Migration (IOM) has warned that Bangladesh suffers severely from both sudden-onset events (e.g. cyclones and floods) and slow-onset events (e.g. sea level rise, saltwater intrusion, and temperature increases). Extensive vulnerability to both has placed enormous stress on both people and resources in this region.

In September 2017, weeks of torrential rain affected more than 8 million people. A full 300,000 were displaced, with over 100,000 homes destroyed and enormous swathes of farmland inundated. Having had to abandon agriculture as a result, many people have moved permanently to urban regions in an attempt to start a new life. However, a present difficulty lies in their blind assumption that they will now be better protected from environmental devastation and will have enhanced economic opportunities to provide for their families. For one thing, overpopulation stemming from such internal migration has massively increased poverty. Over the last 17 years, the slums of Dhaka have drawn in 60 percent more people. Rising sea levels, meanwhile, lead to contamination and create further health issues as water washes away the waste of the slums. Inefficient resource management techniques in turn prevents the capture and storage of excess water, which could otherwise be tapped for a clean and reliable supply.

Magnifying these issues is the fact that Bangladesh has become a safe haven for refugees fleeing atrocities in Myanmar and other climate vulnerabilities in India. The resulting overpopulation is causing excessive competition for acutely limited resources. As the climate worsens, many Rohingya, for example, now face the daunting prospect of being forcibly moved again. The massive Kutupalong refugee camp—home to some 850,000 people—is itself at risk of landslides and flooding, with the monsoon season due to start this month. It is a race against time to reinforce sections of the camp and help its inhabitants to relocate elsewhere. This situation alone could well result in a transfer of thousands more people to the already overstretched capital.

Indeed, Dhaka is nearing its maximum capacity. This means that climate events in the region have an amplified impact. Sadly, as this case demonstrates, millions of migrants are ending up in cities that are even more poorly equipped to withstand the changing climate than the places they have fled. Many, of course, have chosen to remain in their own states. A report by the Environmental Justice Foundation expects tens of thousands of families to become stranded in their own country. Whilst internal migration may be preferable, people are running out of places to move to. Over the coming years, mass international migration will likely be the result, raising concerns of rising cultural hostilities and violence between groups. Whatever approach Bangladesh employs, it must be immediate and far-reaching. Given their lack of resources, international cooperation will be required as the coming years may well prove the most challenging in the country's already troubled history.

Chad: War-Torn and Under-Resourced

Thousands of kilometres away in north-central Africa, Chad likewise suffers from a complex nexus of problems—besides those related to climate change—which render migration especially likely. Perhaps foremost amongst these is impoverishment, with 87 percent of Chadians classified as poor and 63 percent labelled as destitute—the most extreme category of poverty. Economic opportunities are few and far between, with 80–90 percent of the population reliant on agriculture and subsistence farming. Another major challenge is Chad's history of conflict, which has riven the country for 37 out of the past 51 years since independence. Nations that are both poor and conflict-ridden have an extreme lack of adaptive capacity. Their governments are unable to provide access to essential resources, and inhabitants become stranded while trying to provide for themselves.

In this context, climate change is a disrupting factor, one that acts as a threat multiplier. The European Council on Foreign Relations estimated that, in 2012 alone, more than 500,000 people were displaced in Chad as a result. Average temperatures there are rising, causing an increased intensity of catastrophic events. Prolonged droughts, coupled with wasteful irrigation practices, have dried out important natural resources. The Lake Chad Basin, for example—encompassing regions of Niger, Cameroon, Nigeria, and Chadonce covered an area of 25,000 km^2, but only 10 percent of this remains. NASA has estimated that even this could disappear within 25 years. A staggering 2.4 million people have already become displaced, yet this basin remains the lifeblood for a further 38 million, who rely heavily on its water and arable land. The two satellite images below illustrate how depleted the Basin has become over the past 45 years.

Traditionally, livestock farmers have moved to the Sahel region in the north during the rainy season, before later returning back to the south. The drier seasons of recent years have led to a worsening of pastureland and declining crop yields, however, leading to more competition for increasingly limited resources. Conflicts between groups surrounding the Basin are common, and have resulted in more than 7 million people suffering food insecurity. Additionally, the 300,000 Sudanese refugees based in Chad have depleted much of the limited food and water available, creating resentment among the local people.

Globally, the Intergovernmental Panel on Climate Change (IPCC) has found that climate change could cause human displacement through forced migration, while increasing the likelihood of conflict by exacerbating poverty and economic instability. This is especially visible in the case of Chad. As opportunities for livelihoods dwindle or disappear due to failing agriculture, there has been a growing temptation to resort to violence as a means of survival. The Boko Haram crisis in Nigeria has spilled over into Eastern Chad, and there are fears that young, unemployed men will be enticed (or otherwise coerced) into joining in. The Climate Refugees research group found that "climate change, in combination with political, social and development challenges, have affected people's lives, which Boko Haram has capitalised upon to feed its insurgency."

The hapless combination of rampant poverty, overdependence on agriculture, environmental degradation, and population growth in key regions has created an explosive situation in Chad, from which millions are fleeing. Unless immediate steps are taken to improve governance on these issues, migration from Chad and the surrounding Sahel region will increase enormously.

The United States: Hurricanes and Heat Waves

The link between climate change and hurricanes is not new. Indeed, a strong correlation has been demonstrated between warming ocean temperatures, rising sea levels, and a greater intensity of hurricanes. While studies have provided ambiguous results regarding the frequency of hurricanes, it has been shown that their destructive capabilities have increased. Models have predicted a 45–87 percent rise in Category 4 and 5 hurricanes in the US over the last two or three decades. This has been reflected in the damage and displacement such storms have caused in recent years. Hurricane Harvey brought with it more than a million gallons of water per person in Texas, according to some estimates. Over 30,000 people ended up in shelters, with thousands more fleeing further afield in cars. This has become an all-too-familiar exercise for many in the Texas and Louisiana region, who previously experienced and suffered the consequences of Hurricanes Rita (2005) and Ike (2008). As the frequency of these storms increase, along with their destructive capabilities, the prospect of having to rebuild every few years has proven enough to drive people away permanently.

Coastal regions are not the only areas susceptible to flooding and sea level rise. Using climate migration models and data from the IRS, researchers at the University of Georgia found that a 6-foot rise in sea levels caused by excessive emissions would see every state in the US experience climate migration by 2100. The same study asserted that 13 million people are expected to be displaced, with 2.5 million coming from Florida alone; New Orleans will lose a further 500,000 inhabitants, adding to the 100,000 that have already left since the destruction of Hurricane Katrina in 2005. In a further study, the National Oceanic and Atmospheric Association (NOAA) provided a worst-case scenario of an 8.2-foot rise in sea levels by the end of the century. Such an inundation would see the cities of Boston, New York, and Seattle submerged, and many others flooded.

California, meanwhile, has experienced some of the worst droughts and heat waves in its history. We have already witnessed arid areas suffer incredibly destructive forest fires, resulting in thousands of people losing their homes and being forced to relocate permanently. While it is difficult to blame climate change entirely for these events, it certainly exacerbates the problems. Increased temperatures caused by excessive carbon emissions are adding to the already challenging living conditions in the region. Elsewhere, rocketing summer temperatures are causing some parts of the American Southwest to become uninhabitable. In Phoenix last year, temperatures hit 120°F (49°C), rendering it too hot for even planes to fly. Death Valley, meanwhile, breached the 50°C level, with the National Park Service warning visitors to "travel prepared to survive." Such extreme temperatures, if sustained, can cause the rapid onset of heatstroke and lead to death within hours. If emissions stay on their current course, the length and intensity of these weather events is expected to increase dramatically. Resulting migration could cause a mass exodus.

Future predictions for this region make for grim reading. Mass migration resulting from such conditions alone can cause negative impacts extending far beyond mere relocation. The economic implications, for example, are enormous. States such as Arizona and Texas could suffer damages amounting to over 20 percent of their GDP by the end of the century. Northern states, by contrast, are expected to do much better, with areas of Oregon and Washington actually predicted to gain economically.

Those that possess the financial resources to move will probably be able to do so without too much trouble. However, it is conceivable—and even likely—that many others will find it difficult to relocate, and potentially be left behind. This should be cause for significant concern. Studies focusing on the economic damage of a changing climate in the US have suggested that this trend could result in the largest transfer of wealth between rich and poor in history, leading to even higher levels of inequality.

The destination of climate migrants exacerbates the problem. While colder states like Maine may be able to house many displaced people—it has a much lower population density, for example – they too have their limits. Mass migration without the investment in infrastructure to support it would place enormous strain on competition for schools, employment and resources. Comparatively defenceless areas are also becoming migrant hotspots. Florida took in 300,000 people following the recent hurricane in Puerto Rico, and Texas is popular for both internal and transboundary migration from Mexico. Indeed, the cities of Austin, Houston, and Orlando are expected to gain at least 250,000 inhabitants each. As the climate worsens in these areas, there is a high possibility that these migrants will be forced to move again. Landlocked tourist cities such as Las Vegas already suffer from extreme heat and poor resource management; if they are flooded with migrants, they may prove unable to cope with the population growth and ensuing stress on water resources, for example.

The current trajectory of US climate policy is not a good one. The country's withdrawal from the Paris Agreement, coupled with dramatically reduced funding for other climate-related measures such as relocation and housing projects, spells an uncertain future. Moreover, the failure to acknowledge the issue and promote reasonable climate adaptation is extremely dangerous. For example, Florida has passed legislation banning state agencies from mentioning climate change even though they are arguably the most vulnerable state. Continuing to ignore climate change in this manner will greatly aggravate the issue in the future. For

In 2013, Natural Disasters Displaced More People Than War

Natural disasters displaced three times as many people as war last year—even as 2013 was a horrific year for conflict—with 22 million people driven out of their homes by floods, hurricanes and other hazards, a new study has found. "Basically, the combination of mega natural disasters and hundreds of smaller natural disasters massively displaces people in many more countries than the countries that have war and conflict," said Jan Egeland, the secretary of the Norwegian refugee council.

Last year was in some ways an anomaly because so many people were driven out of their homes by war. In some years, 10 times as many people lose their homes to natural disasters. On average, 27 million people a year lost their homes to natural disasters over the last decade. In 2010, that number rose to 42 million.

While mega-disasters such as the devastating typhoon Haiyan in the Philippines attract international attention, the losses due to smaller-scale storms and flooding often go unrecorded. Those living in developing countries are most at risk. The study found more than 80% of those displaced over the last five years lived in Asia. That pattern held last year as well when nearly 19 million of the 22 million displaced lived in Asia.

In many instances, local people do not have time to recover from a disaster before a new one hits, the study found.

The risk of such disasters is also rising, outpacing population growth and even rapid urbanization. Global population has doubled since the 1970s, but the urban population has tripled since that time.

The mass migration from countryside to cities is putting more and more people at risk—especially in Asia's mega-cities, which are the most disaster prone.

Africa, where populations are expected to double by 2050, also faces increasing risk. "These vast urban areas become traps when a natural disaster hits," Egeland said. "People are crammed together and there is no escape. They live in river deltas, they live on hurricane beaches, they live along river beds that are easily flooded, they live where there are mud slides, and so on."

Scientists predict a rise in such extreme weather events in a future under climate change.

"Natural disasters displaced more people than war in 2013, study finds," by Suzanne Goldenberg, Guardian News and Media Limited, September 17, 2014.

the time being, it appears that those most affected will likely be forced to continue navigating the challenges ahead without much assistance from their government.

The Difficulties of Status

Arguments continue regarding the rights of migrants, and definitional dilemmas still plague this discourse. According to the UN's 1951 Convention Relating to the Status of Refugees, a refugee is considered to be someone who is escaping persecution, violence, and/or war. Under this classification, refugees are currently given the right to safe asylum in host countries. However, a debate continues regarding whether climate migrants should be granted a new classification: namely, that of environmental refugees. The reaction to this debate has been mixed. Some argue that refugee status is vital for climate migrants, as it would afford them more rights while attracting attention to the issue. Currently, climate migration is largely under-reported while refugee movements take up the headlines. Granting the status of climate refugee may well serve to sharpen international focus and increase resources to help combat the challenge.

Others categorically reject the proposed label. Many Pacific Islanders have expressed concern that the term under consideration implies helplessness, and carries a certain stigma with which they do not want to be associated. Such cultures feel a deep connection to the lands they inhabit—more so than in most Western societies— territories that have supported their ancestors for thousands of years. While migration may well prove a necessity in the years ahead, those that choose to leave sooner rather than later wish to do so with dignity—something they do not believe the refugee label affords them. Refugee organisations, meanwhile, argue that creating a new status category that encompasses environmental issues would reduce the rights of existing refugees. The United Nations High Commissioner for Refugees (UNHCR)—the UN's refugee agency—has stated that its resources are overstretched already given the ongoing situation in Syria, and would be unable to cope with millions more people without a significant boost in funding.

An unfortunate reality is that the effects of anthropogenic climate change are distributed unequally. It is often the countries producing some of the lowest levels of greenhouse gas emissions (e.g. Bangladesh and Chad) that have been forced to bear the brunt of the ensuing repercussions. This, then, poses an important question of legality versus morality. Climate migrants do not have legal refugee status, but is it fair for states and international organisations to turn their backs on those suffering the impacts of a problem they did little or nothing to cause? This debate is likely to rage on for the foreseeable future. In the meantime, ever-increasing numbers of migrants are fleeing territories that are being rendered uninhabitable due to climate change. If these individuals are unable to gain safe passage—and find a new home—under their current status, a serious consideration of their rights will be necessary. This could mean extending refugee status to cover those affected detrimentally by environmental change, or entail the creation of a new framework altogether.

Certain nations are already taking a proactive approach. New Zealand has announced the creation of a special visa for climate migrants from the Pacific Islands, starting with a limited trial before potentially expanding the program to encompass more people. If successful, this could well set a positive precedent for others to follow.

Conclusion

From Dhaka to Miami, it is almost certain that migration will continue to spike over the coming decades. Unless immediate climate action is taken to keep average temperature increases below the 2°C threshold, we will see cities in Africa overcome by advancing desertification and coastal regions submerged by rising sea levels and increasingly regular natural disasters. Scholars have emphasized the need for migration planning: "whether movement occurs within or between countries, there is a need to prepare for it and in some cases enable it."

Heightened investment would be a logical place to start in adapting to, and mitigating, this challenge. Funding more climate resilient infrastructure projects such as better flood defences would, for example, protect millions from inundation in Bangladesh. Moreover, promoting spending for the development of resource management techniques and enhanced access to water resources in Chad could fortify livelihoods and prevent further violence. The governments in question are unlikely to fund these efforts on their own, but there are many international organisations working to provide assistance for disaster relief and water security. Greater cooperation between these entities is therefore vital.

Bangladesh, Chad, and the United States are all suffering from a lack of climate resilience. They are by no means the only examples. Government research predicts that urban coastal floodplains around the world will see enormous damage over the next three decades, with Asian megacities like Calcutta, Bangkok, and Guangzhou expected to suffer the worst displacement. Nevertheless, status quo-oriented pragmatism is the order of the day. In the face of the massive challenges detailed above, states cannot sit back any longer—they simply do not have the time to continue kicking the can down the road. While it is increasingly impossible to ignore the issue of migration, mitigating its effects is not.

Climate Change and Instability

Carolyn Kenney

In the following viewpoint Carolyn Kenney uses data from a report by the Center for American Progress to show that the changing global climate is beginning to have both humanitarian and economic costs. She also shows how the lack of food and water stability may lead to not only economic effects but also the "weaponizing" of food and water and global political insecurity. She concludes by saying that if countries continue to ignore climate change and its impacts, such as those on critical water and food supplies, the consequences will only become worse. Kenney is a senior policy analyst for National Security and International Policy at American Progress.

As you read, consider the following questions:

1. How has the 2016 US presidential election affected US policies on climate change?
2. What are some of the direct and indirect costs of climate change?
3. How can resources such as water and food be weaponized?

The 2016 US presidential election gave rise to concerns about how the next administration might—or might not—approach the challenges posed by climate change. Unfortunately, thus far, the current administration has not only ignored these challenges

"How Climate Change and Water and Food Insecurity Drive Instability," by Carolyn Kenney, Center for American Progress, November 30, 2017. Reprinted by permission.

but also has taken steps to undermine efforts to combat them, such as announcing the US intention to withdraw from the landmark Paris Agreement, rescinding the Clean Power Plan, and revoking former President Barack Obama's Memorandum on Climate Change and National Security.[1] Presenting one small sliver of hope at this year's Conference of the Parties, acting Assistant Secretary for the Bureau of Oceans and International Environmental and Scientific Affairs in the US Department of State Judith Garber noted that though "the United States intends to withdraw [from the Paris Agreement] at the earliest opportunity, we remain open to the possibility of rejoining at a later date under terms more favorable to the American people."[2] However, the overall picture remains bleak.

The steps back from climate mitigation and response could not come at a worse time, given the rapidly accumulating costs of a changing global climate. As detailed in a previous Center for American Progress report, since 2011, the United States has experienced 84 extreme weather events, which have resulted in some 2,000 deaths and cost a total of roughly $675 billion in damages.[3] Additionally, according to the most recent Global Climate Risk Index, between 1997 and 2016, "more than 524,000 people died as a direct result of more than 11,000 extreme weather events" around the world, which cost about $3.16 trillion in purchasing power parities.[4] These costs, however, are not distributed evenly around the world; they disproportionately fall on the most vulnerable and least equipped to adapt and rebuild. For instance, as the Planetary Security Initiative calculates, from 2004 to 2014, 58 percent of disaster deaths occurred in countries considered to be ranked among the top 30 most fragile states on the Fragile States Index.[5]

Despite the high costs of extreme weather events, investments aimed at reducing the risks posed by climate change abroad have been insufficient. As pointed out in a report by the U.N. High-Level Panel on Humanitarian Financing, for every $100 spent on development aid projects, "just 40 cents has gone into protecting countries from succumbing to natural disasters." Driving the need for investment further, the report notes that "12 out of a group of 23 low-income countries received less than US$ 10 million for DRR [Disaster Risk Reduction] over 20 years while receiving US$ 5.6 billion in disaster response."[6]

This administration has compounded this problem by moving to slash spending on international and domestic institutions and mechanisms that actively work to prevent costly climate and humanitarian crises.[7] However, it is clear that investing in preventive measures, whether they are aimed at conflict prevention or climate change resilience and mitigation, actually reduces costs in the long run. This is true monetarily and, more importantly, in terms of the cost to human lives and livelihoods. The United States should be making strategic investments to build resilience and allay costly future emergency responses—not cutting the already paltry investments in prevention.

In addition to these direct costs, there are also much higher indirect costs associated with climate-induced disasters, especially in fragile states. Climate change acts as a threat multiplier: Weather shocks and their resulting effects can create and exacerbate political, economic, and social tensions—potentially contributing to cycles of poverty, violence, and migration. As pointed out in a previous CAP report,[8] Syria starkly demonstrates this risk. A prolonged drought linked to climate change devastated farming and herding communities in key agricultural regions, leading hundreds of thousands of rural Syrians to move to the cities. While the Syrian war's causes are complex, the dislocation caused by the drought—and the Syrian government's poor response to the crisis—exacerbated social, economic, and political tensions in rural areas and the cities to which many rural families migrated. This discontent underpinned the initial protests and shaped the conditions that led to the outbreak of conflict in 2011 and the resulting refugee crisis. To date, an estimated 465,000 Syrians have been killed and more than 5.3 million Syrians have been displaced.[9]

Ignoring climate change and its effects will take an increasing toll on human lives and livelihoods, economic prosperity, and peace and security. To demonstrate these losses and the real security risks climate change can pose, this issue brief examines the nexus of climate change, water security, and food security in fragile states and highlights some of the threats to international peace and stability that can emerge—specifically, how these issues can drive instability, as well as how water and food are used during conflict as tools for recruitment and weapons of war.

State of Water and Food Security in the World

The most pressing area of concern at the nexus of climate change and national security is water security.[10] As detailed by the World Bank, the effects of climate change have come and will continue to come through the water cycle; droughts, variable or unpredictable rainfall for agriculture or herding, pollution and contamination, and floods or extreme weather can have devastating impacts. The scarcity or surfeit of water can reverberate through crucial systems, affecting food production, pricing, and availability; energy production; transportation and supply chains; densely populated urban areas; and basic environmental systems. These effects will become more severe as populations, cities, and economies continue to grow and strain increasingly limited water resources. The World Bank estimates that roughly 1.6 billion people already live in countries with water scarcity, and that number could double in just two decades.[11]

Directly related to water security is the issue of food security. According to the Food and Agriculture Organization of the United Nations and others, global hunger increased in 2016 following a long decline, affecting 815 million people worldwide, compared with 777 million in 2015.[12] The deterioration of food security was particularly intense in areas experiencing conflict, most notably when compounded by extreme weather events affecting water supplies. Indeed, famine and/or crisis-level food insecurity situations were present in four countries undergoing conflict this year: South Sudan; Nigeria; Somalia; and Yemen.

Climate Change, Water, and Food Supplies as Drivers of Instability

The overlapping incidence of water and food insecurity and conflict is no coincidence; these trends interact with and contribute to one another. The impacts of water and food scarcity can undermine basic livelihoods and exacerbate social tensions, which can lead to instability and conflict if left unaddressed or when compounded by other social or political grievances. The consequences of these intersecting challenges vary greatly around the world as a result of a number of factors, such as political, social, and economic conditions; existing infrastructure; and policy decisions.

For instance, as water and food supplies become constrained, often as a result of extreme weather events spurred by climate change, social tensions over access to available resources can escalate and even turn violent. This is especially dangerous in fragile states that have a history of conflict and in areas where access to these resources has been politicized. The United Nations has found that while disputes over natural resources are rarely the sole driver of violent conflict, they certainly can be a contributing factor when other drivers are present, such as poverty, ethnic polarization, and poor governance.[13] Examples of such disputes can be found all over the world, including in Sudan,[14] Syria,[15] and Yemen,[16] among others.

Water and Food Supplies as Recruitment Tools During Conflict

In the lead-up to and following the eruption of conflicts, resources such as water and food, especially when they are constrained, are often also used as tools for manipulation and recruitment into violent groups. For instance, a recent National Geographic investigation, based on more than 100 interviews with farmers and agricultural officials over three years, concluded that poor government policies and climate-exacerbated drought across rural areas of Iraq and Syria made "many of the most environmentally damaged Sunni Arab villages ... some of the deep-pocketed jihadists' foremost recruiting grounds" for the Islamic State (IS).[17] The report details that with each extreme weather event and harvest loss, recruiters would appear to distribute gifts, such as food or cash, eventually gaining returns on their investments. For instance, near Tikrit, IS gained "much more support from water-deprived communities than from their better-resourced peers." While likely not the sole reason many in these communities joined the ranks of IS, the effects of water and food scarcity and the targeted presentation of alternatives by recruiters seems to have contributed to some decisions to join in these communities.

Water and Food Supplies as Weapons of War

In addition to being used as a recruitment tool, resources such as water and food can be weaponized by armed parties as a way to exert power and exact outcomes over other armed groups and/or civilian populations. For example, U.N. sanctions monitors recently reported to the U.N. Security Council that South Sudan President Salva Kiir and his government "deliberately prevented life-saving food assistance from reaching some citizens." Such actions were described as "amount[ing] to using food as a weapon of war with the intent to inflict suffering on civilians the government views as opponents to its agenda."[18]

Additionally, in Yemen, where almost 7 million are facing famine and 17 million are completely dependent on humanitarian aid, Saudi Arabia implemented a full blockade on all land, air, and sea ports, effectively cutting off critical humanitarian assistance.[19] While the blockade has been partially lifted on ports controlled by Saudi Arabia's allies, humanitarian access is still being blocked in some areas to devastating effect. In addition to the active conflict, what makes the situation in Yemen particularly disastrous is that according to estimates from 2015, the country has the highest level of water scarcity in the world, with at least 50 percent of the population struggling daily to locate or purchase enough safe water to drink or grow their own food.[20]

US and International Community Responses

While it does not appear that the current US administration will do much to address climate change and the threats it poses, the US nonfederal climate movement has flourished. To date, nonfederal climate initiatives and coalitions—which have proliferated in the wake of the Paris Agreement withdrawal announcement—have largely focused on domestic emissions reduction efforts.[21] But city, state, and private sector actors are beginning to recognize that international climate finance and cooperation are essential if they are to take up the mantle of US climate leadership. This was evident in the unprecedented presence of US nonfederal leaders during the 2017 U.N. climate summit in Bonn, Germany. If these nascent nonfederal climate initiatives—such as the US Climate Alliance, for example, which represents nearly 40 percent of the US economy—realize their latent diplomatic power, they could help keep water and food security on the global agenda.

Additionally, as a result of previous legislation, certain US agencies have provided strategy documents on issues related to food and water security, which can provide ready-made blueprints for action when the political will returns at the federal level. Specifically, as mandated by the Senator Paul Simon Water for the World Act of 2014,[22] the US Agency for International Development and the State Department released a Global Water Strategy to the public on November 15, 2017. The strategic objectives listed in the report include the following:

- Increasing sustainable access to safe drinking water and sanitation services, and the adoption of key hygiene behaviors;

- Encouraging the sound management and protection of freshwater resources;

- Promoting cooperation on shared waters; and,

- Strengthening water-sector governance, financing, and institutions.[23]

And while the strategy did not explicitly discuss how climate change will affect water—and by extension, food security—the release of this strategy is an important step forward and will hopefully be fully implemented in the years to come.

International fora for addressing these concerns include the United Nations, the World Bank, both the G-7 and the G-20, and regional bodies such as the European and African Unions. Each of these bodies, through various formats, concluded that climate change poses both direct and indirect threats to human lives and livelihoods, the environment, economic prosperity, and international peace and security. As such, they have taken steps to try to combat climate change—through the signing of the historic Paris Agreement,[24] the U.N. Sustainable Development Agenda,[25] and initiatives such as the G-7's report and platform on climate and fragility risks[26] and the G-20's Agricultural Market Information System (AMIS).[27] However, more work will be needed in the future, especially absent US federal leadership.

Conclusion

For conflict-prone countries, particularly those most affected by climate change, it is critical to understand how strains on water and food supplies can overlap to drive instability and conflict. Climate impacts can disrupt livelihoods, contribute to decisions to migrate, and exacerbate social tensions. Access to scarce food and water supplies can also be used as a recruitment tool by violent groups, and even harnessed as a weapon of war. If individuals continue to ignore climate change and its impacts, such as those on critical water and food supplies, the consequences will only grow more dire. In a global environment of increasing uncertainty, it is essential to not only change behaviors that perpetuate climate change but also work to build more resilience to and mitigate the inevitable impacts the world will face as a result.

Notes

1. Madison Park, "6 Obama climate policies that Trump orders change," CNN, March 28, 2017, available at http://www.cnn.com/2017/03/28/politics/climate-change-obama-rules-trump/index.html.

2. US Department of State, "U.S. National Statement at COP-23: Remarks, Judith G. Garber," November 6, 2017, available at https://www.state.gov/e/oes/rls/remarks/2017/275693.htm.

3. Kristina Costa, Miranda Peterson, and Howard Marano, "Extreme Weather, Extreme Costs: How Our Changing Climate Wallops Americans' Wallets" (Washington: Center for American Progress, 2017), available at https://www.americanprogress.org/issues/green/reports/2017/10/27/441382/extreme-weather-extreme-costs/.

4. David Eckstein, Vera Kunzel, and Laura Schafer, "Global Climate Risk Index 2018" (Bonn, Germany: Germanwatch, 2017), available at https://germanwatch.org/en/download/20432.pdf.

5. William Ligtvoet and others, "Water, climate and conflict: security risks on the increase?" (Planetary Security Initiative and others, 2017), available at https://www.clingendael.org/publication/water-climate-and-conflict-security-risks-increase.

6. The High-Level Panel on Humanitarian Financing, "Too important to fail—addressing the humanitarian financing gap" (2016), available at https://reliefweb.int/sites/reliefweb.int/files/resources/%5BHLP%20Report%5D%20Too%20important%20to%20fail%E2%80%94addressing%20the%20humanitarian%20financing%20gap.pdf.

7. CAP National Security and International Policy Team, "President Trump's Proposed Budget Is Bad for U.S. National Security," Center for American Progress, March 1, 2017, available at https://www.americanprogress.org/issues/security/news/2017/03/01/427139/president-trumps-proposed-budget-is-bad-for-u-s-national-security/; Gwynne Taraska and Howard Marano, "The Perversity of Cutting the International Climate Budget," Center for American Progress, March 16, 2017, available at https://www.americanprogress.org/issues/green/news/2017/03/16/428450/perversity-cutting-international-climate-budget/.

8. Carolyn Kenney, "Climate Change, Water Security, and U.S. National Security" (Washington: Center for American Progress, 2017), available at https://www.americanprogress.org/issues/security/reports/2017/03/22/428918/climate-change-water-security-u-s-national-security/.

9. Reuters Staff, "Syrian War Monitor Says 465,000 Killed in Six Years of Fighting," Reuters, March 13, 2017, available at https://www.reuters.com/article/us-mideast-crisis-syria-casualties/syrian-war-monitor-says-465000-killed-in-six-years-of-fighting-idUSKBN16K1Q1; U.N. High Commissioner for Refugees, "Syrian Regional Refugee Response: Inter-agency Information Sharing Portal," available at http://data.unhcr.org/syrianrefugees/regional.php (last accessed November 2017).

10. Kenney, "Climate Change, Water Security, and U.S. National Security."

11. World Bank Group, "High and Dry: Climate Change, Water, and the Economy." Working Paper (2016), available at https://openknowledge.worldbank.org/handle/10986/23665.

12. Food and Agriculture Organization of the United Nations and others, "The State of Food Security and Nutrition in the World" (2017), available at http://www.fao.org/3/a-I7695e.pdf.

13. The United Nations Interagency Framework Team for Preventive Action, "Renewable Resources and Conflict: Toolkit and Guidance for Preventing and Managing Land and Natural Resources Conflict" (2012), available at http://www.un.org/en/land-natural-resources-conflict/renewable-resources.shtml.

14. Ibid.
15. Francesco Femia and Caitlin Werrell, "Climate Change Before and After the Arab Awakening: The Cases of Syria and Libya." In Caitlin E. Werrell, Francesco Femia, and Anne-Marie Slaughter, eds., "The Arab Spring and Climate Change: A Climate and Security Correlations Series" (Washington: Center for American Progress, 2013), available at https://www.americanprogress.org/issues/security/reports/2013/02/28/54579/the-arab-spring-and-climate-change/.
16. Collin Douglas, "A Storm Without Rain: Yemen, Water, Climate Change, and Conflict," Center for Climate and Security, August 3, 2016, available at https://climateandsecurity.org/2016/08/03/a-storm-without-rain-yemen-water-climate-change-and-conflict/.
17. Peter Schwartzstein, "Climate Change and Water Woes Drove ISIS Recruiting in Iraq," *National Geographic*, November 14, 2017, available at https://news.nationalgeographic.com/2017/11/climate-change-drought-drove-isis-terrorist-recruiting-iraq/.
18. Michelle Nichols, "Exclusive: South Sudan's government using food as weapon of war—U.N. report," Reuters, November 10, 2017, available at https://www.reuters.com/article/us-southsudan-security-un-exclusive/exclusive-south-sudans-government-using-food-as-weapon-of-war-u-n-report-idUSKBN1DA2OX.
19. The Editorial Board, "Saudis Try to Starve Yemen Into Submission," The *New York Times*, November 16, 2017, available at https://www.nytimes.com/2017/11/16/opinion/saudi-arabia-yemen-famine.html.
20. Frederika Whitehead, "Water scarcity in Yemen: the country's forgotten conflict," The Guardian, April 2, 2015, available at https://www.theguardian.com/global-development-professionals-network/2015/apr/02/water-scarcity-yemen-conflict.
21. Gwynne Taraska and Howard Marano, "Advancing the U.S. Nonfederal Movement to Support the Paris Agreement" (Washington: Center for American Progress, 2017), available at https://www.americanprogress.org/issues/green/reports/2017/11/06/442233/advancing-u-s-nonfederal-movement-support-paris-agreement/.
22. Senator Paul Simon Water for the World Act of 2014, Public Law 289, 113th Cong., 2d sess. (December 19, 2014), available at https://www.congress.gov/bill/113th-congress/house-bill/2901.
23. US Government, "U.S. Government Global Water Strategy" (2017), available at https://www.usaid.gov/sites/default/files/documents/1865/Global_Water_Strategy_2017_final_508v2.pdf.
24. U.N. Framework Convention on Climate Change, "The Paris Agreement," available at http://unfccc.int/paris_agreement/items/9485.php (last accessed November 2017).
25. United Nations, "Sustainable Development Goals," available at http://www.un.org/sustainabledevelopment/sustainable-development-goals/ (last accessed November 2017).
26. "A New Climate for Peace—Taking Action on Climate and Fragility Risks," available at https://www.newclimateforpeace.org/ (last accessed November 2017).
27. Agricultural Market Information System, "Home," available at http://www.amis-outlook.org/home/en/ (last accessed November 2017).

In the Pacific Islands Hotspots for Climate Migrants Require Further Research

John Campbell and Olivia Warrick

In the following excerpted viewpoint John Campbell and Olivia Warrick argue that the Pacific islands have already begun to experience the consequences of climate change. Climate change can cause a reduction in land, livelihood, or habitat security for some Pacific communities, and in many cases, island inhabitants are already being forced to migrate to areas because their homes and livelihoods are no longer sustainable. Many of these refugees move to urban areas, but rural to urban migration and population growth strains the capacity of urban areas. And as urban populations continue to grow there is likely to be an increased demand from urban populations for international migration. Campbell is Associate Professor at the Department of Geography, University of Waikato, New Zealand. Warrick is Senior Pacific Climate Advisor at Red Cross Red Crescent Climate Centre.

"Climate Change and Migration Issues in the Pacific," by John Campbell and Olivia Warrick, International Labour Organization (ILO), August 2014. Reprinted by permission.

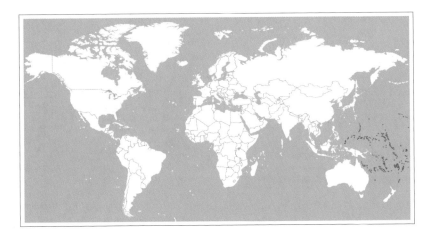

As you read, consider the following questions:

1. Why are Pacific populations especially at risk from climate change?
2. What are the five Pacific "hotspots"?
3. What is the current pattern of migration? How might it change?

Climate change has significant implications for Pacific island populations, many of whom reside in coastal areas and rely on natural resources for their livelihoods and well-being. Climate change impacts may affect internal or even international migration flows as some island environments become less able to support the communities that depend on them.

The linkages between climate change and migration are only beginning to gain recognition. There have been a few studies on climate change and migration conducted in the Pacific; however, the methodology used across studies has not been consistent and the studies have also not been linked with policy interventions. This report provides a synthesis of the current information available on climate change and migration in the Pacific. It also identifies information gaps in the existing knowledge base.

Environmental change can contribute to individual's decision to migrate. Although economic and social reasons may be the primary reasons for migration, environmental change can also contribute to the decision to migrate. Climate change can cause a reduction in land, livelihood or habitat security for some Pacific communities. For example, low-lying coastal areas and river deltas may become unsuitable for physical settlement, or they remain habitable but income and food security options become marginal; or reduced precipitation or increased disease vectors could cause the deterioration of habitability. The impacts of climate change can be the tipping point which results in an individual or family deciding to migrate.

In the longer term, the planned relocation of some communities may be required, particularly in areas where population density and growth rates are high. In the shorter term, the voluntary migration of individuals and households could aid in relieving environmental pressure when coupled with improved in situ adaptation strategies, population management and climate-resilient development.

There are five "hotspots" in the Pacific that are likely to become source areas for climate change-related migrants: (a) urban areas; (b) urban atolls; (c) non-urban atolls; (d) coastal, delta and riverine communities; and (e) communities prone to drought. As cited by the International Organization for Migration (IOM), global estimates for the number of migrants moving due to climate change range between 25 million and 1 billion people by 2050, with 200 million people the most commonly cited figure. Inherent uncertainties mean that only rough estimates can be given for the number of people likely to be involved in migration related to climate change. However, the impacts of climate change on migration will be more acute in particular habitats.

A review of the existing literature identifies five localities that are potential "hotspots" requiring increased research into climate change impacts, in situ adaptation responses, demographic processes and community security. These include: (a) urban areas; (b) urban atolls; (c) non-urban atolls; (d) coastal, delta and riverine communities; and (e) communities prone to drought. Unmanaged rural to urban migration and population growth strains the capacity of urban areas to cope with the impacts of climate change; as urban populations continue to grow there is likely to be an increased demand from urban populations for international migration. Both urban and non-urban atolls are particularly vulnerable to climate change impacts and the impact of development pressure on the environment. It is difficult to separate many of the impacts of climate change from the impacts of development on the environment of atolls, both result in salt water intrusion, a decline in Ocean health and coastal erosion. Coastal areas have high vulnerability to the projected climate change related increased severity of coastal hazards and the degradation of ocean-based livelihoods. River deltas are highly vulnerable to flooding which is likely to increase due to climate change. Additionally, there are many drought prone areas in the Pacific where increased drought may result in increased migration demand (this includes the Highlands of Papua New Guinea, as well as atolls and coastal areas).

Climate change is likely to increase the demand for both internal and international migration opportunities. Migration is likely to follow current patterns in the immediate term. The voluntary movement of individuals and families is likely to be towards labour market opportunities, including rural to urban migration. In larger Pacific island countries, climate change may predominately impact internal migration and urbanization; however, in small countries, territories and atolls, the subsequent exacerbation of urban areas may increase interest in international migration. Some Pacific island countries have access agreements with Australia, New Zealand and the United States of America, which already host large diasporas. However, many of those countries that may have the greatest potential migration pressures, including Tuvalu, Kiribati and Nauru, have the fewest international destination options.

Voluntary migration of individuals and communities can be adaptive if it is well managed. Internal migration or international labour migration can enhance the adaptive capacity of the migrant-sending community through the generation of remittances, reduced population pressure on homeland environments, and in the case of circular migration, the transfer of knowledge and skills. Labour migration can also fill human resource gaps in the receiving community. However, unplanned migration can result in unemployed migrants, negative remittances and social problems.

There are many economic, social, cultural and psychological costs associated with climate change-related migration.

Historical examples of the costs of environmental migration point to the loss of tradition, language, identity, livelihoods and community cohesion. Additionally, the viability of homeland communities may be compromised if too many people move. The costs of both displacement and voluntary climate change-induced migration are likely to increase with greater distances from traditional homelands. Social, cultural and psychological costs may be experienced even in cases of internal migration.

The planned resettlement of entire communities, either within a country or internationally, may be required in some instances; however, the cultural and social impacts of community relocation may be severe. Climate change-forced displacement is highly disruptive to livelihoods, culture and society unless proper, well-planned interventions support people in their effort to adapt to the challenges. Although migration is a normal part of life for many Pacific communities, accepting migration as an adaptive response to climate change is often associated with a threat to sovereignty and cultural identity.

There are significant information gaps in understanding the impacts of climate change on migration in the Pacific.

Particular research needs include: the integration of climate change and migration policy; costs of climate change-related migration on sending and receiving communities; gendered implications of voluntary and forced climate change-related migration; and the role of remittances in adaptive capacity.

[...]

Periodical and Internet Sources Bibliography

The following articles have been selected to supplement the diverse views presented in this chapter.

Lisa Cornish, "Climate change's impact on migration is strong and growing." Devex, March 12, 2018. https://www.devex.com/news/climate-change-s-impact-on-migration-is-strong-and-growing-92246

Simon Davies, "Climate change may cause human migration in Bangladesh." Berkeley ESPM, June 12, 2018. https://ourenvironment.berkeley.edu/news/2018/06/climate-change-may-cause-massive-human-migration-bangladesh

Fiona Harvey, "Devastating climate change could lead to 1m migrants a year entering EU by 2100." Guardian, December 21, 2017. https://www.theguardian.com/environment/2017/dec/21/devastating-climate-change-could-see-one-million-migrants-a-year-entering-eu-by-2100

Silja Klepp, "Climate Change and Migration." Oxford Research Encyclopedias, 2018. http://climatescience.oxfordre.com/view/10.1093/acrefore/9780190228620.001.0001/acrefore-9780190228620-e-42

Vally Koubi and Thomas Bernauer, "How Climate Change Affects Migration." ETH Zurich, February 10, 2018. https://www.ethz.ch/en/news-and-events/eth-news/news/2018/02/bernauer-koubi-climate-change-migration.html

Kelly M. McFarland and Vanessa Lide, "The effects of climate change will force millions to migrate. Here's what this means for human security." *Washington Post*, April 23, 2017. https://www.washingtonpost.com/news/monkey-cage/wp/2017/04/23/the-effects-of-climate-change-will-force-millions-to-migrate-heres-what-this-means-for-human-security/?utm_term=.c2dc8f1d1d82

Laura Parker, "143 Million People May Soon Become Climate Migrants." *National Geographic*, March 19, 2018. https://news.

nationalgeographic.com/2018/03/climate-migrants-report-world-bank-spd/

Benjamin Schraven, "Climate Change Is Not Everything—The Causes Of Flight And Migration Are Manifold." German Development Institute, June 6, 2017. https://www.die-gdi.de/en/the-current-column/article/climate-change-is-not-everything-the-causes-of-flight-and-migration-are-manifold/

Andrea Thompson, "Wave of Climate Migration Looms, but It 'Doesn't Have to Be a Crisis.'" *Scientific American*, March 23, 2018. https://www.scientificamerican.com/article/wave-of-climate-migration-looms-but-it-doesnt-have-to-be-a-crisis/

UCLA, "Migration, Immigration, And Climate Change." UCLA Re-Imagining Migration. https://reimaginingmigration.org/migration-immigration-and-climate-change/

United Nations, "Climate Change Is A Key Driver of Migration and Food Insecurity." United Nations Framework Convention on Climate Change, October 16, 2017. https://unfccc.int/news/climate-change-is-a-key-driver-of-migration-and-food-insecurity

GLOBALVIEWPOINTS

CHAPTER 3

The Politics of Climate Change

In the United States Climate Adaptation Plans Vary

Lykke Leonardsen

As climate change begins to affect parts of the United States, large cities, especially on the East Coast, are studying the potential impact of extreme weather on their infrastructure. In the following excerpted viewpoint, Lykke Leonardsen presents a case study of Philadelphia and how it is implementing policies and plans for adapting to and coping with climate change, both now and in the future. The author highlights the importance of planning and working together across governmental departments to cope with the coming changes. Leonardsen is the head of the Climate Unit, in charge of the Climate Change Adaptation program, and the city's ambitious plan to be the first carbon neutral capital of the world before 2025.

As you read, consider the following questions:

1. Why is Philadelphia a good case study for climate change adaptation?
2. If Philadelphia is experiencing a period of new growth, why is it especially important to study climate change there?
3. Why is stormwater management an important issue in this city?

"Implementation of Climate Change Adaptation Solutions in U.S. Cities," by Lykke Leonardsen, The German Marshall Fund of the United States, June 22, 2017. Reprinted by permission.

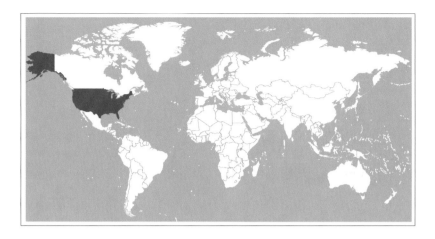

ocated on the Delaware River on the East Coast of the United States, Philadelphia is the fifth largest city in the United States with a population of more than 1.5 million residents and over six million in the greater metropolitan area. Philadelphia is a port city and lies at the intersection of two rivers.

Philadelphia has one of the highest poverty rates and a very low tax base. Although the economic and social context is beginning to improve with new investment and residents, the city still struggles financially. Nonetheless, Philadelphia is a case which proves that innovation and political courage can make a difference.

Expected Impacts of Climate Change

Compared to the West Coast, cities on the East Coast face the prospect of more severe impacts as a result of climate change. The greatest risks are rising sea levels and an increase in intense rainfall and heat.

Some of the consequences associated with climate change have already started to happen. Since 2010, the city has experienced many challenges:[14]

- The snowiest winter ever

- The two warmest summers ever

- The most days over 90 degrees ever
- The warmest July ever
- The wettest month ever
- The wettest year ever
- Two hurricanes

These recent weather experiences show that climate change needs to be taken seriously, especially in a city that is currently experiencing a new period of growth after decades of decline. It is also a challenge given the city's capacity issues and ongoing economic and social challenges.

Organization

Philadelphia's financial challenges come into relief when analyzing the city's work on sustainability. The Office for Sustainability has only six full-time staff, and like other US cities, their main function is to coordinate work that takes place in other departments in the city or outside city government. The Office's main task is to ensure other city departments integrate sustainability and climate change adaptation into their work.

The city has developed an ambitious sustainability plan, called Greenworks. Published in 2009, Greenworks was developed under the former director of the Office for Sustainability, Mark Alan Hughes, a professor from Penn State University, who, at the request of the Mayor Michael Nutter, developed the plan. Though climate change adaptation does not figure directly in the plan, green stormwater management is one of the plan's central strategies.[15]

Additionally, the city's Office for Sustainability has included climate change adaptation strategies into their work—especially since Sandy in 2012. This work culminated in a report *Growing Stronger* published in December 2015 that addresses both climate change and possible adaptation strategies.[16]

Actions

One of the issues concerning climate change in Philadelphia is the risk of more frequent storms and, as a result, higher levels of precipitation. That is primarily why stormwater management has a high priority in the city and why it drives the local sustainability agenda. Faced with demands from the EPA to reduce overflows from the combined sewer system, and to some extent build on the lessons from Portland, the city in 2011 launched the plan "Green City-Clean Waters," in which the city proposed moving from grey infrastructure to green infrastructure. One of the arguments for this was the business case. A grey infrastructure-based solution would have cost in the vicinity of 8 billion dollars, while the green infrastructure solution cost much less, amounting to less than 3 billion dollars.

Philadelphia's ambitious green infrastructure plan is an example of the holistic thinking that is also driving the city's policy agenda. While this thinking might be driven by a lack of city funds, it will ultimately add quality to the urban landscape, create climate benefits, and manage stormwater at the same time, as was indicated by city representatives interviewed for this project.

Philadelphia also has a few examples where thinking across sectors has created new opportunities for the implementation of green infrastructure projects. One example is the public schools where a project to create new green schoolyards was combined with stormwater management strategies. In this way, stormwater management can co-finance part of the project, making it possible to rebuild more schoolyards and handle more water at the same time. Unlike New York, Portland and Seattle, climate change adaptation is much more present in the city's day-to-day operations. The city is working on an ambitious outreach program to property owners and residents in flood zones. Indeed, the city is able to provide financial support for installing sewer backflow prevention in basements because they are able to prove the business case as explained above for making such changes.

Beyond these efforts, the work of climate adaptation in Philadelphia is only in the beginning stages. The Mayor's Office of Sustainability and the Delaware Valley Regional Planning Agency have been working directly with the various sectors, posing key questions: How will changes in the weather pattern affect individual residents? How much will certain types of interventions cost a resident? What can residents do to prevent damages? These interviews have formed part of the basis of what has now been published in the report *Growing Stronger*.

Lessons Learned

There are two primary lessons from Philadelphia that can be applied to the Copenhagen context. First, a lot can actually be achieved with very little money. Integrated planning and thinking can go a long way in achieving citywide impact by making sure that every dollar spent is spent in such a way that it impacts more than one purpose.

Secondly, it is important for cities to take time to craft and develop thoughtful strategies because this allows for more thorough responses. The City of Copenhagen has been in a hurry to implement adaptation techniques as a result of recent severe flooding. This means the City has not been able to carry out a detailed sectoral risk and vulnerability assessment as a city like Philadelphia has already begun to do.

Notes

14. US Environmental Protection Agency, "Climate Change Adaptation in Philadelphia," April 17, 2013, http://www.epa.gov/statelocalclimate/documents/pdf/april-17-4-climate-change-adaptation-in-philadelphia.pdf.
15. City of Philadelphia, Pennsylvania, "Making Philadelphia Greener," http://www. phila. gov/green/greenworks/pdf/Greenworks_OnlinePDF_FINAL.pdf.
16. City of Philadelphia, Pennsylvania, "Making Philadelphia Greener," http://www. phila. gov/green/pdfs/Growing%20Stronger.pdf.

Climate Refugees Are Being Ignored in the Discussions About Displaced People

Tim McDonnell

In the following viewpoint Tim McDonnell argues that although diplomats from around the world are meeting to discuss displaced people, they are not paying enough attention to climate refugees. Currently, there is no international agreement on who should qualify as a climate refugee and no plan for managing the growing crisis. There is no formal recognition of climate refugees, or even a formal definition. The author argues that recognition and protection of these refugees under international law is vital and must happen now. McDonnell is a journalist covering the environment, conflict, and related issues in sub-Saharan Africa.

As you read, consider the following questions:

1. Why don't climate refugees receive the same attention as political refugees?
2. If the majority of today's climate refugees are displaced within the borders of their own country, how does this affect those countries?
3. What types of programs are presented as possibly helping reduce the need for climate migration?

"The Refugees the World Barely Pays Attention To," by Tim McDonnell, NPR.org, June 20, 2018. Reprinted by permission.

This month, diplomats from around the world met in New York and Geneva to hash out a pair of new global agreements that aim to lay out new guidelines for how countries should deal with an unprecedented surge in the number of displaced people, which has now reached 65.6 million worldwide.

But there's one emerging category that seems to be getting short shrift in the conversation: so-called "climate refugees," who currently lack any formal definition, recognition or protection under international law even as the scope of their predicament becomes more clear.

Since 2008, an average of 24 million people have been displaced by catastrophic weather disasters each year. As climate change worsens storms and droughts, climate scientists and migration experts expect that number to rise.

Meanwhile, climate impacts that unravel over time, like desert expansion and sea level rise, are also forcing people from their homes: A World Bank report in March projects that within three of the most vulnerable regions—sub-Saharan Africa, South Asia and Latin America—143 million people could be displaced by these impacts by 2050.

In Bangladesh, hundreds of thousands of people are routinely uprooted by coastal flooding, many making a treacherous journey to the slums of the capital, Dhaka. In West Africa, the almost total disappearance of Lake Chad because of desertification has empowered terrorists and forced more than four million people into camps.

It's a problem in the United States as well. An estimated 2,300 Puerto Rican families displaced by Hurricane Maria are still looking for permanent housing, while government officials have spent years working to preemptively relocate more than a dozen small coastal communities in Alaska and Louisiana that are disappearing into the rising sea.

A December study by Columbia University climate researchers in the peer-reviewed journal *Science* projected that if global temperatures continue their upward march, applications for asylum to the European Union could increase 28 percent to nearly 450,000 per year by 2100.

But so far, there's no international agreement on who should qualify as a climate refugee—much less a plan to manage the growing crisis.

"These people fall through the cracks," says Erol Yayboke, a development expert at the Center for Strategic and International Studies who helped author a May report on forced migration. "It's hard for countries to come to a consensus on something like this."

That difficulty took shape during the second and third weeks of June in the latest round of negotiations on the Global Compact for Migration and the Global Compact on Refugees, which are due to be adopted at the U.N. General Assembly this fall.

When the compacts were first proposed in 2016, there was some hope among migration researchers and advocates that they could provide a platform for new international policies on climate refugees, which had gained prominence since the 2015 Paris climate talks. But that hope was quashed in March, when Louise Arbour, the U.N. official leading the migration compact—which, of the two agreements, was considered the more likely venue for strong climate language—told the European Union that the document would not grant "specific legal international protection to climate-induced migrants."

Both compacts do make some reference to the climate. The latest draft of the migration compact calls on U.N. members to "better map, understand, predict and address migration movements, including those resulting from sudden- and slow-onset natural disasters, environmental degradation, the adverse effects of climate change" and "cooperate to identify, develop and strengthen solutions, including planned relocation and visa options" for climate migrants.

The refugee compact stops much shorter, only mentioning climate as one of many factors that "may interact with the drivers of refugee movements."

Ideally, the compacts should encourage countries to create new legal processes to document and manage climate migrants "so people can move before the water is literally lapping at their feet," says Nina Hall, a migration expert at Johns Hopkins University. As an example, she cited a plan in New Zealand to offer up to 100 special climate visas to Pacific Islanders—although that process is still in development and isn't likely to open for several years, she said.

But the language in the compacts is too vague to spur much progress, she says, and in any case neither compact will be legally binding.

"We have to be up front that the global compacts are not going to transform the landscape for climate migrants," Hall says.

Climate refugees pose a number of unique challenges for international policymakers compared to those displaced by persecution, the traditional driver recognized by the 1951 UN Refugee Convention. While some people, like the Puerto Ricans displaced by Maria, are affected by a specific disaster, many others are forced to move because of slow-onset changes like sea level rise and desertification, which can make it hard to identify them as climate refugees. Researchers are still working to understand how climate change interacts with the panoply of other factors, including national security and local economic trends, that might prompt a family to move.

At the same time, the majority of today's climate refugees are displaced within the borders of their own country, whereas the new compacts focus exclusively on cross-border movement. And for Pacific island nations that face a truly existential threat from sea level rise, there's no legal precedent to guide how they might relocate to new territory in another country—if they even want to move. Even a comparatively simpler effort—to relocate a community of fewer than 100 people in Louisiana whose island home, Isle de Jean Charles, has lost 98 percent of its land to sea level rise since the 1950s, to a new town 40 miles inland—has taken several years and cost $50 million and still faces setbacks,

Climate Change Refugees Are Our Responsibility

Australia needs to plan for an influx of climate change refugees from neighbouring countries that face ever increasing risks from cyclones, rising sea levels and more severe droughts, according to a researcher at the University of Technology, Sydney (UTS).

Fears about waves of mass migration from climate change are unfounded, says the university's Elaine Kelly. But Dr Kelly, a UTS Chancellor's Post Doctoral Research Fellow, says Australia should start planning migration streams that include people who have lost their homes to climate change, in addition to those we already accept for other humanitarian reasons.

"The reality is climate change will provoke more displacement, and displacement of those who are most poor," says Dr Kelly. "How are we going to plan for that?"

"We need to think about local, regional and international ways of regulating migration if we want to do it well," says Dr Kelly.

Dr Kelly argues that because climate change is increasing the pressure for people living in south-east Asia to migrate to safer regions, it is more important than ever that the debate about migration, and particularly about refugees, should be based on ethics rather than politics or national security.

Most climate change adaption will be local, says Dr Kelly. For example, migration from low-lying rural areas in Bangladesh to the capital, Dhaka, is expected to increase the city's population to 40 million by 2050 from 15 million today.

Dr Kelly has observed a sense of hospitality in the international refugee program for those suffering political persecution, a sense sorely lacking in Australia.

"Hospitality to affected countries from the industrial countries responsible for climate change must be seen as either a mode of adaptation or a form of compensation for profound losses and damages caused by climate change," she says.

"I would love to see a reasoned discussion of [the ethics of climate change] in Australia, one that isn't polemic and isn't driven by fear. I'd love to see a discussion that looks at the human issues and at the pragmatic approaches that government can take."

"Climate change refugees are our responsibility," by Åsa Wahlquist, Phys.org, February 18, 2014.

including complaints from the predominantly Native American residents that the state government didn't adequately involve them in the planning process.

"The reality is there are tens of millions of these people, and we don't agree on what we can do about them," Yayboke says.

Meanwhile, the wave of nationalism and anti-immigrant sentiment that has swept across Europe and the US in recent years has made it a challenge for the U.N. to even get governments to follow existing refugee protocol, let alone expand it to cover an entirely new class of refugee, Hall says.

"To get any progressive international policy, much less hard law, is almost impossible in today's climate," she says. "We're not going to get any kind of binding convention on displaced people due to climate change."

The US pulled out of the migration compact in December, citing concerns that it could impede the Trump administration's immigration agenda. While that means the final agreement will be missing any commitment from the world's number-one migrant destination, it does remove a potential roadblock to including climate-specific language, given Trump's disbelief in climate change.

In any case, the global compacts aren't the end of the issue. A different U.N. task force that was established in the Paris climate agreement is set to deliver a new set of recommendations on climate refugees around the same time the compacts are adopted. They will likely focus on measures individual countries can take to prevent climate refugees from being displaced in the first place, says Mariam Traore Chazalnoel, a climate expert at the U.N.'s International Organization for Migration.

"Most people don't actually want to migrate," she says. "They would rather stay where they are. But they need the means to stay where they are."

That could include programs to train and equip farmers for drought tolerance, she says, raise homes out of flood plains, and other measures aimed at increasing communities' resilience to climate shocks. Yayboke believes that development agencies need to step up funding for climate adaptation programs, which can help prevent displacement and reduce government spending on recovery from predictable natural disasters later on.

"We are spending so much money on this stuff, but we're being totally reactive," he says. "There are proactive things we can do that we're just not doing."

Few places are more illustrative of that problem than Bangladesh. According to the CSIS report, up to 70 percent of the five million people living in Dhaka's slums were displaced from their original home by environmental disasters.

"The situation and scope of this problem is entirely new, and of biblical proportions," says Steve Trent, executive director of the Environmental Justice Foundation, which released its own report on Bangladesh in 2017. "It demands an entirely new legal convention. The global compacts are a start, but it's clear that they're not enough."

Developed Countries Must Do More Than Reduce Emissions

Shyam Saran

In the following viewpoint, written just before the Paris climate change summit of 2015, Shyam Saran argues that as the world considers reducing its carbon emissions, it is vital to make a distinction between the "survival" carbon needs of developing countries and the "lifestyle" uses of carbon in developed countries. Each country must come to the summit with the intention to contribute as much as it can and take away as little benefit to itself as possible, because everyone is faced with an urgent and global challenge. Saran is a former foreign secretary of India. He was India's chief negotiator on climate change from 2007 to 2010.

As you read, consider the following questions:

1. What will happen to developing countries if developed countries do not make efforts to reduce their carbon emissions?
2. Climate negotiations should be about countries working together to reduce emissions. What have they largely been instead?
3. What is one suggestion for countries to cooperatively address climate change?

"Paris climate talks: Developed countries must do more than reduce emissions," by Shyam Saran, Guardian News and Media Limited, November 23, 2015. Reprinted by permission.

We are only days away from the climate change summit in Paris. Several world leaders are likely to be present to applaud a successful outcome, which is virtually guaranteed since the bar has been set so low in terms of effort expected from the major industrialized economies.

Under the UN process which the negotiations have been taking place, countries are required only to present their climate pledges (known as Intended Nationally Determined Contributions, or INDCs, which are voluntary and subject to an international review but with no strict compliance procedure).

It is this pledge and review system which will become the template for future climate change action. Past experience shows that such weak international regimes, which posit only a best endeavour commitment, rarely deliver expected results.

The UN recently reported that aggregating all the INDCs so far, the world would be on a trajectory of 2.7C, when a 2C rise is already the limit of safety defined by scientists.

What many people fail to realize is that global warming is the consequence of the stock of greenhouse gas emissions, chiefly CO2, which has accumulated in the Earth's atmosphere as a result of fossil fuel based industrial activity in the industrialized countries of the world.

This is the reason why the UN recognizes the historical responsibility of the developed countries in causing global warming even though current industrial activity in major developing countries such as China and, to a much lesser extent, India is adding incrementally to that stock.

If developed countries do not make significant and absolute reductions in their emissions there will be a progressively smaller carbon space available to accommodate the development needs of developing countries. There is a difference between the emissions of developing countries which are "survival" emissions and those of developed countries which are in the nature of "lifestyle" emissions.

They do not belong to the same category and cannot be treated on a par.

To blur this distinction is to accept the argument that because "we got here first, so we get to keep what we have, while those who come later must stay where they are for the sake of the saving the planet from the threat of climate change." Far from accepting their historical responsibility developed countries are instead trying to shift the burden on to the shoulders of developing countries.

This they have been doing by keeping attention focused on current emissions while ignoring the source of the stock of emissions in the atmosphere. A sustainable and effective climate change regime cannot be built on the basis of such inequity.

One often hears the argument that it is all very well to preach equity but given the planetary emergency the world faces from the threat of climate change we must set aside the equity principle in the interests of humanity as a whole. This is a wholly specious and self serving argument. It reflects the sense of entitlement to an affluent lifestyle, based on energy intensive production and consumption, while denying the even modest aspirations of people in developing countries.

In a densely interconnected and globalised world, it will be impossible to maintain islands of prosperity in an ocean of poverty and deprivation. It is not that developing countries are claiming the right to spew as much carbon as possible into the atmosphere without regard to the health of the planet.

As the main victims of climate change—the impacts of which they are already suffering—they have a much bigger stake in dealing with this challenge. They are, in fact, doing much more than most developed countries, to adopt energy frugal methods of growth, conserving energy, promoting renewable power and limiting waste within the limits of their own resources.

They could do much more if they had access to finance, technology and capacity building from developed countries, a commitment which is incorporated in the UN. Success may elude Paris if developed countries continue to evade their responsibility to provide adequate financial resources and transfer appropriate technologies to developing countries to enable them to enhance their own domestic efforts.

Climate negotiations have become less about meeting an elemental challenge to human survival and more about safeguarding narrowly conceived economic self interests of nations. These are negotiations conducted in a competitive frame, where each party gives as little as possible and extracts as much as possible. The inevitable result is a least common denominator result and this is what is expected at Paris.

Imagine if each country came with the intention to contribute as much as it can and take away as little benefit to itself as possible, because we are all faced with an urgent and global challenge. We would then get a maximal outcome—which is what the world requires if it has to escape the catastrophic consequences of climate change. The negotiating dynamic may change dramatically.

The leaders can capture the imagination of people around the world if they explicitly acknowledge the seriousness of the threat we all confront and commit themselves to a global collaborative effort to deal with it based on the principle of equitable burden sharing.

Why not create a global technology platform which brings together the best minds from developed and developing countries alike to create new climate-friendly technologies which can then be disseminated as global public goods? Given the promise of solar power, why not announce a global solar mission designed to make it a mainstream energy source in a decade? Since coal will continue to be a major source of power generation in many countries of the world, could we collaborate together on a clean coal mission which reduces harmful emissions and increases the efficiency of coal combustion?

Countries can then contribute according to their capacities and resource availability and I have no doubt that emerging countries such as India, China or Brazil will be enthusiastic participants in such initiatives. Even if we are unable at this stage to go beyond the INDCs which have already been submitted the adoption of these initiatives may reassure the world that a new and more promising process has been set in motion to deliver a more sustainable future for our common home.

Adopting Smarter Policies Will Allow Communities to Adapt to Changes from Climate Change

Alice Thomas

In the following viewpoint, an interview with Alice Thomas, Thomas argues that the limited definition of a refugee does not allow those displaced because of climate change to claim asylum. However, most such migrants are actually moving within their own countries. The author contends that state governments and the international community can prepare for such crises by enacting policies to allow for smoother adaptation. Thomas is program manager for climate displacement at Refugees International.

As you read, consider the following questions:

1. What does the World Bank predict for "trapped population" by the year 2050?
2. How is environmental displacement different now as compared to the past according to the viewpoint?
3. What country has emerged as a leader in assisting climate refugees according to the viewpoint?

"Q&A with Alice Thomas, Climate Refugee Expert," South Africa Today, August 16, 2018. https://southafricatoday.net/environment/qa-with-alice-thomas-climate-refugee-expert/ Licensed under CC BY ND 4.0 International. This article first appeared on Mongabay https://news.mongabay.com/2018/08/not-doing-anything-is-no-longer-acceptable-qa-with-alice-thomas-climate-refugee-expert/.

In many ways, 2018 is the year of the refugee. At US borders, Mediterranean shores and Asian cities, millions are fleeing war, hunger and persecution in search of safety and shelter. And scientists believe things will only get worse due to climate change.

The Office of the United Nations High Commission for Refugees (UNHCR) estimates that rising seas, intensifying droughts and other extreme weather events will uproot 250 million people by 2050. Like most other refugees, climate refugees are expected to come largely from developing nations in Africa, Asia and South America. But unlike those escaping war and persecution, climate refugees have few legal protections.

"The 1951 Refugee Convention's definition of 'refugee' does not include people who are fleeing environmental stress," says Alice Thomas, the climate displacement program manager at the nonprofit group Refugees International (RI). To date, no individual has been able to successfully claim asylum on the grounds that they are fleeing climate change, Thomas says, though some have tried.

And there is another climate reality, according to Thomas, that is rarely recognized: the fact that most climate-affected migrants will not be leaving their countries.

"International migration is really complex. Most people, the poorest people, can't afford to migrate internationally," she says. "There needs to be focus on these what we call 'trapped populations'; people who are too poor to even move and escape climate effect."

A 2018 World Bank report suggests that these trapped populations might number over 140 million people by 2050. That's why Thomas says countries worldwide need an internal migration policy. Such policies should help people who need to move and resettle within their own nation so they are not stateless. Smart climate change adaptation policies may even make it possible so that people don't have to move in the first place.

"They need to build resilience to more drought. They need to build houses that are hurricane and flood proof," Thomas says. "That's why it's the poorest people who are most affected. People living in informal homes or shacks in Bangladesh or Haiti or even in Puerto Rico are among those who will be worst-affected and most likely to be compelled to move."

Thomas has been working on these very issues for nearly a decade. In an interview with Bhanu Sridharan for Mongabay, the former environmental lawyer breaks down the issue of climate migration and steps that need to be taken both internationally and by individual nations to help the most vulnerable adapt to a crisis not of their making.

Mongabay: How did you become interested in climate change and the potential for climate change to lead to migration and the refugee crisis?

Alice Thomas: I am an environmental lawyer. I have practiced international environmental law and policy for most of my career. When Refugees International decided to start this program, there really weren't any other organizations at that time [2009] that were focused on the need to do advocacy around the human impacts of climate change, specifically on displacement and migration. I was very interested in this job because I was very interested in defending communities who were vulnerable to climate change and because those who were most likely to be impacted were those who had the least responsibility for the climate crisis.

Can you tell us a little bit more about Refugees International? What is your organization's objective with regard to climate migration?

Refugees International is an independent nongovernment organization that advocates for improved assistance and protection for refugees, those who are displaced internally within their own countries, and who are displaced by other events like climate change, disasters and gang violence. The organization has been around for almost four decades advocating for refugees around the world. It is a totally independent organization. We don't take any U.N. funding and we don't take any government funding. And that allows us to advocate fiercely only on behalf of displaced people who are our constituents.

RI's climate displacement program is focused on different countries that are experiencing climate stress. One goal has been to improve international protection for people who are forced to flee their home countries because of climate change. The other goal has been to find ways to improve the response to people who are displaced by extreme weather or climate change-related effects.

Human beings have been moving because of environmental changes for millennia. What is the difference between that and the climate migration we see today?

Well, it's true that people have been moving for millennia. Migration has always been an adaptation strategy for people who are experiencing environmental stress. To this day, in large parts of Africa, pastoralists move because they need to go where there's pasture and there's water.

The problem with climate change is that it takes us outside the historic bounds of weather and climate ranges that people have adapted to over millennia. It's taking us into extremes beyond what's normal. People can't adapt to those changes fast enough.

For example, in Africa, especially the Sahel region and the Horn of Africa, people are extremely vulnerable to even minor changes in weather and climate. They are extremely poor and depend solely on rain-fed agriculture to survive. Their planting seasons correspond to rainy seasons that occur maybe twice a year. Once it starts raining, they'll plant and harvest their crop. But now what they are seeing—and I've witnessed this when I visited—is that the patterns of rain are no longer normal. The rains will start on time, and they will go out and plant, but then the rains will just stop, and their crops will wither and die. These changes in rainfall patterns can affect their ability to grow food. And because it's outside the normal pattern, they can't predict or plan for it.

Most people use the term "climate refugee." But people who are displaced by environmental events can't claim asylum or protection as refugees right now. Why is that?

That's correct. The 1951 Refugee Convention's definition of "refugee" does not include people who are fleeing environmental stress. Other regional conventions could potentially cover people who are fleeing climate change-related effects. But there haven't been any cases that I am aware of where people have been granted asylum only on the grounds that they were fleeing climate change. There was one case in New Zealand where someone from [the islands of] Kiribati tried to claim asylum on that ground. But the court found that there was not a sufficient showing of climate impacts on that person to qualify for asylum.

Your organization has been engaged in the development of the U.N. Global Compact on Refugees and Migration recently. Was this issue raised in the meeting? Are there steps being taken now to correct this?

There are actually two global compacts happening in parallel. One is a Global Compact on Refugees and the other is a Global Compact on Migration. The Refugees Compact is limited in scope to refugees as defined under the 1951 Convention. So it will not end up being a document that would broaden the definition of a refugee to include persons forced to flee the effects of climate change. And that's not what it was trying to do. It was trying to address the current refugee crisis. But it acknowledges that there may be forms of mixed movement where people may be trying to flee both conflict and the effects of climate change.

The Global Compact on Migration is a different beast. It is setting out new (non-binding) commitments by governments around the world with respect to international migration. There is consensus in the room among U.N. member states that there needs to be cooperation on how to address the issue of climate- and disaster-induced migration. And there's recognition that the countries that are going to be the worst impacted by this, especially small island developing states, really need to have new opportunities for migration for their people.

What sorts of solutions are being looked at with small island developing states?

The small island developing states have been for a long time—gosh, probably more than a decade—asking the international community to do something about the risk that they are facing. They have brought this issue to the U.N. Human Rights Council and there's recognition that this is a violation of their peoples' human rights and a threat to their existence. But there's been no real solution to this.

We are now aware that the impacts of climate change are already locked in for small island states. Given that reality, they are now urging the international community to support them to adapt to those effects, including expanding legal migration pathways.

What role does the Paris Agreement play in dealing with this issue?

Climate change as a driver of migration and displacement has been recognized earlier by the Conference of Parties (COP) to the U.N. climate convention. The Paris accord set up a task force in late 2015 to look at measures to avert, minimize and address climate displacement. The task force is now working to develop a set of recommendations that it will be sharing at the upcoming climate talks in Poland, at the end of this year. And countries need to start looking at those recommendations and adopting them in their national plan of action. And we need to ensure that countries that need financial assistance to implement those measures get financial assistance.

Refugees are increasingly unwelcome in big developed nations like the US and parts of the EU. Do these countries have a different stance on climate migrants?

The US has traditionally been and continues to be the lead donor for humanitarian assistance globally. However, the current administration's proposed budget sought to slash humanitarian aid and that's including to countries that have been the worst affected by climate change. Luckily, we continue to have bipartisan support in Congress for humanitarian assistance programs. So proposals by the administration to significantly cut back humanitarian aid have been rejected and humanitarian support maintained, although it is still nowhere near as much as is needed.

But we still need to see more investment for disaster risk reduction and much more for climate change adaptation. Even under former administrations, [the US] hadn't done enough to help countries adapt to climate change, but it was making an effort. Under this administration we have seen funding for climate change adaptation zeroed out.

Europe in this time period has really stepped up a lot in dealing with climate mitigation and humanitarian assistance, but unfortunately they do not have a very friendly refugee or migration policy right now. Canada has emerged as a real leader in all ways.

A lot of migration is internal, i.e. people moving within their own country. Are you concerned about that aspect as well? Or are you only concerned when people have to leave their nation-state and move to another country?

Right now, the evidence shows that most people [affected by climate change] will migrate or be displaced internally. So it needs to be addressed. And I feel there is a lot of opportunity in the coming decade to prevent this sort of migration. To help people who don't want to move and stay in place adapt.

But for those migrating, we also need to prepare for that as well. Part of the problem is that there's no policy for internal migration in most countries. This has all come to a head in Alaska, where impoverished indigenous communities want to relocate because the Arctic is warming so quickly. There are dozens of native Alaskan communities that want to move inland, because they are literally falling into the water as the permafrost melts beneath them. They don't even want to move very far inland. But there is no legal or administrative framework to do that. They don't have federal or state funds to set up infrastructure in advance of their move. So this lack of policies and laws for internal migration is also a very big gap right now.

Do you think focusing on poverty alleviation or infrastructure in the countries impacted may help?

Fighting poverty will help, but all of our policies, whether humanitarian strategies or development strategies, need to incorporate climate change. They need to do things differently than they did in the past. They need to build resilience to more drought. They need to build houses that are hurricane- and flood-proof. That's why it's the poorest people who are most affected. People living in informal homes or shacks in Bangladesh or Haiti or even in Puerto Rico are among those who will be worst-affected and most likely to be compelled to move.

Are there any wealthy communities that have also been forced to move because of climate stress?

It's almost always that poor communities don't have the resources to move and those are the people we are focused on. But if you look at Hurricane Katrina [in New Orleans], you had a city with both poor and rich communities. A lot of wealthy people with means who lost their homes in the storm were able to rebuild their homes to better standards or they just went somewhere else. They were able to find what we call a "durable solution" to their displacement. What the evidence shows is that the people who didn't find a durable solution to displacement were poor African-American communities living in the Lower Ninth ward.

I think that after disasters, wealthy people are able to rebuild or move. They did so in the Florida Keys after Hurricane Irma and in Puerto Rico. But the people who lived in the trailer parks in the Keys, I don't know what happened to those people.

I think the issue of climate migration garnered a lot of attention because of the Syrian crisis, the idea that a drought led to the civil war and that led to displacement. What do you think?

With respect to Syria, I haven't analyzed the situation myself, but I think the literature shows that it hasn't been firmly established that there was a direct link between the drought and civil war. And that corresponds to the broader literature. There are not many cases where climate events, like droughts, directly led people to pick up arms and go to war with each other. Rather, the evidence shows that climate-related disasters can lead to other forms of social stress or mental stress. They can also aggravate pre-existing tension. Where societies are predisposed to racial or ethnic tensions, climate change can aggravate the situation.

Are there any examples of this?

Well, in Somalia there's been another very protracted drought and more than 800,000 people have been internally displaced. And there the terrorist organization Al-Shabaab has been taking advantage of this and intimidating people who need food and water. They have been blocking humanitarian aid from coming into affected areas.

Mostly this doesn't sound like a cheerful job. Are you optimistic that progress will be made?

As much as I have been frustrated by the slow pace of action, the fact that you're seeing this climate displacement task force within the UNFCCC and the Global Compacts on Migration and Refugees trying to create international cooperation on this, represents important progress. When I started eight years ago, we didn't have that. So we have seen that discussions have moved; states have moved. Even in a really bad political climate, even in a xenophobic political climate, even in an anti-refugee political climate, we have seen common sense and human morality prevail. Not doing anything is no longer acceptable.

The Costs and Consequences of Climate Change on Our World Will Define the 21st Century

Michael Werz and Laura Conley

In the following viewpoint Michael Werz and Laura Conley state that the issue of climate change will define the 21st century as the world is forced to deal with the effects of a warming climate as well as trying to decrease its causes. Countries will also have to address the implications of climate change on political conflict and security, as well as humanitarian and military aid. The article also provides examples of how the global security of the United States could be affected. Werz is a senior fellow at the Center for American Progress, where his work as a member of the National Security Team focuses on the nexus of climate change, migration, and security and emerging democracies, especially Turkey, Mexico, and Brazil. Conley is an attorney and former foreign policy analyst for the Center for American Progress.

As you read, consider the following questions:

1. Why do the authors feel that the issue of climate change will "define" the 21st century?
2. How does climate change affect global stability and the possibility for global conflict?
3. How could climate change affect US global security?

"Climate Change, Migration, and Conflict," by Michael Werz and Laura Conley, Center for American Progress, January 3, 2012. Reprinted by permission.

The costs and consequences of climate change on our world will define the 21st century. Even if nations across our planet were to take immediate steps to rein in carbon emissions—an unlikely prospect—a warmer climate is inevitable. As the U.N. Intergovernmental Panel on Climate Change, or IPCC, noted in 2007, human-created "warming of the climate system is unequivocal, as is now evident from observations of increases in global average air and ocean temperatures, widespread melting of snow and ice and rising global average sea level."

As these ill effects progress they will have serious implications for US national security interests as well as global stability—extending from the sustainability of coastal military installations to the stability of nations that lack the resources, good governance, and resiliency needed to respond to the many adverse consequences of climate change. And as these effects accelerate, the stress will impact human migration and conflict around the world.

It is difficult to fully understand the detailed causes of migration and economic and political instability, but the growing evidence of links between climate change, migration, and conflict raise plenty of reasons for concern. This is why it's time to start thinking about new and comprehensive answers to multifaceted crisis scenarios brought on or worsened by global climate change. As Achim Steiner, executive director of the U.N. Environment Program, argues, "The question we must continuously ask ourselves in the face of scientific complexity and uncertainty, but also growing evidence of climate change, is at what point precaution, common sense or prudent risk management demands action."

In the coming decades climate change will increasingly threaten humanity's shared interests and collective security in many parts of the world, disproportionately affecting the globe's least developed countries. Climate change will pose challenging social, political, and strategic questions for the many different multinational, regional, national, and nonprofit organizations dedicated to improving the human condition worldwide. Organizations as different as Amnesty International, the US Agency for International Development, the

World Bank, the International Rescue Committee, and the World Health Organization will all have to tackle directly the myriad effects of climate change.

Climate change also poses distinct challenges to US national security. Recent intelligence reports and war games, including some conducted by the US Department of Defense, conclude that over the next two or three decades, vulnerable regions (particularly sub-Saharan Africa, the Middle East, South and Southeast Asia) will face the prospect of food shortages, water crises, and catastrophic flooding driven by climate change. These developments could demand US, European, and international humanitarian relief or military responses, often the delivery vehicle for aid in crisis situations.

This report provides the foundation and overview for a series of papers focusing on the particular challenges posed by the cumulative effects of climate change, migration, and conflict in some of our world's most complex environments. In the papers following this report, we plan to outline the effects of this nexus in northwest Africa, in India and Bangladesh, in the Andean region of South America, and in China. In this paper we detail that nexus across our planet and offer wide-ranging recommendations about how the United States, its allies in the global community, and the community at large can deal with the coming climate-driven crises with comprehensive sustainable security solutions encompassing national security, diplomacy, and economic, social, and environmental development.

Here, we briefly summarize our arguments and our conclusions.

The Nexus

The Arab Spring can be at least partly credited to climate change. Rising food prices and efforts by authoritarian regimes to crush political protests were linked first to food and then to political repression—two important motivators in the Arab makeover this past year.

To be sure, longstanding economic and social distress and lack of opportunity for so many Arab youth in the Middle East and across North Africa only needed a spark to ignite revolutions across the region. But environmental degradation and the movement of people from rural areas to already overcrowded cities alongside rising food prices enabled the cumulative effects of long-term economic and political failures to sweep across borders with remarkable agility.

It does not require much foresight to acknowledge that other effects of climate change will add to the pressure in the decades to come. In particular the cumulative overlays of climate change with human migration driven by environmental crises, political conflict caused by this migration, and competition for more scarce resources will add new dimensions of complexity to existing and future crisis scenarios. It is thus critical to understand how governments plan to answer and prioritize these new threats from climate change, migration, and conflict.

Climate Change

Climate change alone poses a daunting challenge. No matter what steps the global community takes to mitigate carbon emissions, a warmer climate is inevitable. The effects are already being felt today and will intensify as climate change worsens. All of the world's regions and nations will experience some of the effects of this transformational challenge.

Here's just one case in point: African states are likely to be the most vulnerable to multiple stresses, with up to 250 million people projected to suffer from water and food insecurity and, in low-lying areas, a rising sea level. As little as 1 percent of Africa's land is located in low-lying coastal zones but this land supports 12 percent of its urban population.

Furthermore, a majority of people in Africa live in lower altitudes—including the Sahel, the area just south of the Sahara—where the worst effects of water scarcity, hotter temperatures, and longer dry seasons are expected to occur. These developments may well be exacerbated by the lack of state and regional capacity to manage the effects of climate change. These same dynamics haunt many nations in Asia and the Americas, too, and the implications for developed countries such as the United States and much of Europe will be profound.

Migration

Migration adds another layer of complexity to the scenario. In the 21st century the world could see substantial numbers of climate migrants—people displaced by either the slow or sudden onset of the effects of climate change. The United Nations' recent Human Development Report stated that, worldwide, there are already an estimated 700 million internal migrants—those leaving their homes within their own countries—a number that includes people whose migration is related to climate change and environmental factors. Overall migration across national borders is already at approximately 214 million people worldwide, with estimates of up to 20 million displaced in 2008 alone because of a rising sea level, desertification, and flooding.

One expert, Oli Brown of the International Institute for Sustainable Development, predicts a tenfold increase in the current number of internally displaced persons and international refugees by 2050. It is important to acknowledge that there is no consensus on this estimate. In fact there is major disagreement among experts about how to identify climate as a causal factor in internal and international migration.

But even though the root causes of human mobility are not always easy to decipher, the policy challenges posed by that movement are real. A 2009 report by the International Organization for Migration produced in cooperation with the United Nations University and the Climate Change, Environment and Migration Alliance cites numbers that range from "200 million to 1 billion migrants from climate change alone, by 2050," arguing that "environmental drivers of migration are often coupled with economic, social and developmental factors that can accelerate and to a certain extent mask the impact of climate change."

The report also notes that "migration can result from different environmental factors, among them gradual environmental degradation (including desertification, soil and coastal erosion) and natural disasters (such as earthquakes, floods or tropical storms)." Clearly, then, climate change is expected to aggravate many existing migratory pressures around the world. Indeed associated extreme weather events resulting in drought, floods, and disease are projected to increase the number of sudden humanitarian crises and disasters in areas least able to cope, such as those already mired in poverty or prone to conflict.

Conflict

This final layer is the most unpredictable, both within nations and transnationally, and will force the United States and the international community to confront climate and migration challenges within an increasingly unstructured local or regional security environment. In contrast to the great power conflicts and the associated proxy wars that marked most of the 20th century, the immediate post-Cold War decades witnessed a diffusion of national security interests and threats. US national security policy is increasingly integrating thinking about nonstate actors and nontraditional sources of conflict and instability, for example in the fight against Al Qaeda and its affiliated groups.

Climate change is among these newly visible issues sparking conflict. But because the direct link between conflict and climate change is unclear, awareness of the indirect links has yet to lead to substantial and sustained action to address its security implications. Still the potential for the changing climate to induce conflict or exacerbate existing instability in some of the world's most vulnerable regions is now recognized in national security circles in the United States, although research gaps still exist in many places.

The climate-conflict nexus was highlighted with particular effect by the current US administration's security-planning reviews over the past two years, as well as the Center for Naval Analysis, which termed climate change a "threat multiplier," indicating that it can exacerbate existing stresses and insecurity. The Pentagon's latest Quadrennial Defense Review also recognized climate change as an "accelerant of instability or conflict," highlighting the operational challenges that will confront US and partner militaries amid a rising sea level, growing extreme weather events, and other anticipated effects of climate change. The US Department of Defense has even voiced concern for American military installations that may be threatened by a rising sea level.

There is also well-developed international analysis on these points. The United Kingdom's 2010 Defense Review, for example, referenced the security aspects of climate change as an evolving challenge for militaries and policymakers. Additionally, in 2010, the Nigerian government referred to climate change as the "greatest environmental and humanitarian challenge facing the country this century," demonstrating that climate change is no longer seen as solely scientific or environmental, but increasingly as a social and political issue cutting across all aspects of human development.

As these three threads—climate change, migration, and conflict—interact more intensely, the consequences will be far-reaching and occasionally counterintuitive. It is impossible to predict the outcome of the Arab Spring movement, for example, but the blossoming of democracy in some countries and the demand for it in others is partly an unexpected result of the consequences of climate change on global food prices. On the other hand, the interplay of these factors will drive complex crisis situations in which domestic policy, international policy, humanitarian assistance, and security converge in new ways.

Areas of Concern

Several regional hotspots frequently come up in the international debate on climate change, migration, and conflict. Climate migrants in northwest Africa, for example, are causing communities across the region to respond in different ways, often to the detriment of regional and international security concerns. Political and social instability in the region plays into the hands of organizations such as Al Qaeda in the Islamic Maghreb. And recent developments in Libya, especially the large number of weapons looted from depots after strongman Moammar Qaddafi's regime fell—which still remain unaccounted for—are a threat to stability across North Africa.

Effective solutions need not address all of these issues simultaneously but must recognize the layers of relationships among them. And these solutions must also recognize that these variables will not always intersect in predictable ways. While some migrants may flee floodplains, for example, others may migrate to them in search of greater opportunities in coastal urban areas.

Bangladesh, already well known for its disastrous floods, faces rising waters in the future due to climate-driven glacial meltdowns in neighboring India. The effects can hardly be over. In December 2008 the National Defense University in Washington, D.C., ran an exercise that explored the impact of a flood that sent hundreds of thousands of refugees into neighboring India. The result: the exercise predicted a new wave of migration would touch off religious conflicts, encourage the spread of contagious diseases, and cause vast damage to infrastructure.

India itself is not in a position to absorb climate-induced pressures—never mind foreign climate migrants. The country will contribute 22 percent of global population growth and have close to 1.6 billion inhabitants by 2050, causing demographic developments that are sure to spark waves of internal migration across the country.

Then there's the Andean region of South America, where melting glaciers and snowcaps will drive climate, migration, and security concerns. The average rate of glacial melting has doubled over the past few years, according to the World Glacier Monitoring Service. Besides Peru, which faces the gravest consequences in

---

Climate Change and Poor Countries

The international community must do more to help low-income countries cope with the climate change, says the IMF in its "World Economic Outlook" report to be released next month.

"Advanced and emerging market economies have contributed the lion's share to actual and projected warming," argues the IMF. "Helping low-income countries cope with its consequences is both a moral duty and sound global economic policy."

Low-Income Countries Bear the Brunt

With an unprecedented increase in global temperatures over the past 40 years, and significant further warming predicted unless greenhouse gas emissions are massively reduced, low-income countries are set to suffer the worst of the extreme droughts, floods and rising sea levels that will result—even if their emissions are relatively low.

"The Earth's warming affects countries very unequally," say the authors of the report in the IMF Blog. "Even though low-income countries have contributed very little to greenhouse gas emissions, they would bear the brunt of the adverse consequences of rising temperatures, since they tend to be situated in some of the hottest parts of the Earth."

Countries in Africa, Asia and Central and South America will feel the effects of rising temperatures more than most.

Latin America, a number of other Andean countries will be massively affected, including Bolivia, Ecuador, and Colombia. This development will put water security, agricultural production, and power generation at risk—all factors that could prompt people to leave their homes and migrate. The IPCC report argues that the region is especially vulnerable because of its fragile ecosystem.

These four regions of the world—northwest Africa, India and Bangladesh, the Andean region, and China—will require global, regional, and local policies to deal with the consequences of climate change, migration, and conflict.

Finally, China is now in its fourth decade of ever-growing internal migration, some of it driven in recent years by

Economies in hot countries will be affected on various levels, including lower agricultural yields, reduced worker productivity, slow investment, and damaged health. Close to 60 percent of the world's population currently resides in countries that are vulnerable to such climate change consequences—a number that's projected to rise to 75 percent by the end of the century.

Climate Change-Induced Conflict and Migration

If higher temperatures potentially cause more natural disasters, this will also fuel greater conflict and migration, argues the IMF.

"The cross-border spillovers from these impacts of climate change in vulnerable countries could be very sizable, and advanced economies will not be immune either."

Nonetheless, the report also cites research that shows that migration is largely limited to those who can afford to travel; and that people in low-income developing countries are generally trapped amid weather disasters triggered by climate change.

"Given the constraints faced by low-income countries, the international community must play a key role in supporting these countries' efforts to cope with climate change—a global threat to which they have contributed little," say the IMF.

"Climate change burden unfairly borne by world's poorest countries,"
by Stuart Braun, Deutsche Welle, September 28, 2017.

environmental change. Today, across its vast territory, China continues to experience the full spectrum of climate change-related consequences that have the potential to continue to encourage such migration. The Center for a New American Security recently found that the consequences of climate change and continued internal migration in China include "water stress; increased droughts, flooding, or other severe events; increased coastal erosion and saltwater inundation; glacial melt in the Himalayas that could affect hundreds of millions; and shifting agricultural zones"—all of which will affect food supplies.

These four regions of the world—northwest Africa, India and Bangladesh, the Andean region, and China—will require global, regional, and local policies to deal with the consequences of climate change, migration, and conflict. Alas, such policies that might be effective in these complex crisis environments cannot be designed within the existing global institutional framework. There are many reasons for this.

In the United States, as in many other developed nations, the defense, diplomacy, and economic and social development silos are not adept at analyzing the input of a broad range of policy fields in combination with direct dialogue with the people of the affected regions. From Europe's perspective, the fragmented nature of the continent's reaction to rising climate migrants from Africa stands out. From the perspective of regional powers such as India, China, Brazil, and South Africa, there are yet again different sets of policy priorities that block action. And from the perspective of multilateral organizations, there is another set of policy disconnects.

Yet action is critical. Environmentally induced migration, resource conflicts, and unstable states will not only have an impact upon the nations where they occur, but also on the United States and the broader international community.

Moving Forward

The interplay of migration, climate change, and conflict is complex and will be with us for the long term. Nevertheless, the uncertainty surrounding the exact causality should not be a reason for ignoring this key nexus. And while the causal relationship may not always be clear, the lines of inquiry moving forward are becoming apparent. To understand this nexus, we will need to ask, for example, what role mediating factors such as economic opportunity, levels of development, health indicators, and legal status will play in the relationship between climate change and migration. It will be equally critical to determine whether there is a threshold at which the effects of climate change could be significant enough to cause migration directly, or at what level of climate change it will become the most important of several migration "push" factors.

Additionally, we should ask whether climate change will alter the composition of migrant communities. Migrants, after all, are not necessarily the most desperate or destitute of their countrymen and women. Migrations, particularly across international borders, often require means. Could a significant increase in extreme weather events or long-term shifts in climate norms alter this dynamic, and what would be the implications of that shift?

Some instances of the complete climate, migration, and conflict nexus exist to guide the examination of these questions. Consider, for example, the Second Tuareg Rebellion in Mali in 1990. British economist Nicholas Stern argues that drought in Mali in the decades preceding the conflict contributed to local and international migration. Those who later tried to return found a "lack of social support networks for returning migrants, continuing drought, and competition for resources between nomadic and settled people," all of which were among the factors that sparked the rebellion.

Jeffrey Mazo at the International Institute of Strategic Studies adds that the forced migration ultimately pushed some young men into Algeria and Libya, "where many were radicalized"—a dangerous development in an already unstable region. In past months refugees from Qaddafi's former regime in Libya have been taking refuge with the Tuareg along the borders of Libya, Algeria, and Mali.

Imagine similar migration-fueled conflicts in India and Bangladesh, the Andean region, and in China. We can't know how they might develop but we do know the three ingredients— climate change, migration, and conflict. From the perspective of a forward-looking policymaker, situations like this suggest that the uncertainty that still surrounds the climate, migration, and conflict nexus requires greater attention when it comes to security solutions, not less.

In this paper and the reports to follow, we will discuss regional case studies in which the cumulative effects of climate change, migration, and conflict interact within a broad framework of political, economic, and environmental security challenges. Our objective is to develop a robust contemporary notion of sustainable security that effectively integrates defense, diplomacy, and development into a comprehensive policy designed to deal with today's global threats while preventing future threats from occurring.

We delve into these recommendations in detail at the end of this paper but in this section we briefly explain how we believe the international community, the United States, its allies, and key regional players can together create a sustainable security situation to deal with climate change, migration, and conflict. Specifically they must:

- Conduct federal government institutional reform in the United States that addresses the development-security relationship and that prioritizes planning for long-term humanitarian consequences of climate change and migration as a core national security issue

- Develop strategies to strengthen intergovernmental cooperation on transboundary risks in different regions of the world

- Increase funding for the Global Climate Change Initiative

- Ensure better information flows and more effective disaster response for early-warning systems

- Support the best science to expand our understanding of specific circumstances such as desertification, rainfall variability, disaster occurrence, and coastal erosion, and their relation to human migration and conflict

- Identify regions most vulnerable to climate-induced migration, both forced and voluntary, in order to target aid, information, and contingency-planning capabilities

- View migration as a proactive adaptation strategy for local populations under pressure due to increased environmental change

A truly sustainable approach to security, then, requires us not only to look at the traditional security threats posed by the interaction between states, but also to understand that the security of the United States is advanced by promoting the individual well-being of people across the developing world, and by embracing collective responses to shared threats posed by climate change. We turn first to understanding the dynamics of those threats.

We Must Listen to Climate Refugees Now

Rebecca Buxton and Theophilus Kwek

In the following viewpoint Rebecca Buxton and Theophilus Kwek argue that scientists, politicians, and concerned citizens are focusing too much on the long-term effects of climate change. That isn't wrong; however, they are too distracted to notice there is a more immediate problem in front of them: those displaced by the effects of climate change. The authors contend that these refugees must be heard now. Buxton is a student at Oxford University, reading for an MSc in Refugee and Forced Migration Studies. Kwek was formerly vice president of the Oxford Students' Oxfam Group. He is also reading for the MSc in Refugee and Forced Migration Studies at Oxford University.

As you read, consider the following questions:

1. Why do the authors open with mention of Donald Trump's presidential victory?
2. How many of the Solomon Islands have been submerged in the past year according to the authors?
3. Why aren't climate refugees given the attention they need according to the viewpoint?

"Losing Ground: Listening to the Voices of Climate Refugees," by Rebecca Buxton and Theophilus Kwek, Open Migration, February 8, 2017. https://openmigration.org/en/op-ed/losing-ground-listening-to-the-voices-of-climate-refugees/. Licensed under CC BY 4.0 International.

Following Donald Trump's victory in last November's election, more people are concerned about the planet than ever before. Polls on the eve of his inauguration reveal a clear increase in the number of Americans who believe that their own families—in addition to many in developing countries—will be harmed by the effects of climate change. Equally, scientists around the world have voiced outrage against the President's repeated denials of global warming as well as new, heavy-handed "crackdowns" on US government science agencies.

While this groundswell of public awareness and activism is encouraging, we risk overlooking the ever-more precarious position of the already-existing climate refugees around the world. Predictions of New York and London being submerged in a matter of decades have long captured headlines. But the current effects of climate change in countries such as Bangladesh, Kiribati, Tuvalu, and the Solomon Islands, where homes and livelihoods have already been lost, hardly feature in the recent outcry. By focusing exclusively on the long-term effects of air pollution or ocean acidification, protestors and politicians alike risk freezing the voices—and choices—of today's climate refugees out of the debate.

The Consequences of Trump's Policies on Climate Refugees

It's hard to ignore the adverse impacts that Trump's policies will have on climate refugees, not least the US's impending withdrawal from the Paris Agreement. Myron Ebell, climate change denier and leader of the transition team for the Environmental Protection Agency, has said that the President is resolved to undo the commitments to reduce greenhouse gases made by Barack Obama in 2015. He also stated that an executive order to this effect could be rolled out within "days," and this is worrying for several reasons.

First, other signatories to the Paris Agreement are likely to default on their commitments. Though these states are unlikely to formally retract, the loss of political pressure from the US may allow states to vastly overstep their carbon quotas, and overall effects on the environment will reach far beyond just America's failed commitment alone. Second, even if Trump's successor carries out large-scale environmental reform, the carbon footprint generated under this administration may well tip global warming past the point of no return. The Intergovernmental Panel on Climate Change argues that if global average temperatures rise above 2°C, changes to the atmosphere will be abrupt and irreversible, and new policies will have to adapt to, rather than prevent, climate catastrophe.

In combination, these consequences have massive effects for sea-level rise. Six partially eroded islands in the Solomons have already been submerged in the past year, with some UN predictions claiming that 15% of Pacific islands will disappear with under one meter of sea-level rise. Unfortunately, without US leadership, resettlement plans for those displaced from these islands are unlikely to come to fruition.

The Broader and Deep-Seated Tendency to Deprioritize Climate Refugees

But at-risk communities have not only been threatened by Trump's recent policies. The dangers they face are also exacerbated by a more deep-seated tendency among rich donor states and the development community alike to focus on displaced persons in conflict zones, or refugees at their doorsteps. As early as 2008, commentators were referring to climate refugees as "the forgotten people," routinely left out of conversations about refugee issues— especially in the absence of legal recognition, or any long-term resettlement plans by the UNHCR. Despite urgent warnings last year by the Obama administration, lives affected by climate change remain very much a "forgotten narrative." Even those who study the issue tend to spotlight long-term risks for larger countries over current losses faced by small ones, while hotly-contested political campaigns on both sides of the Atlantic have centred on refugees fleeing war and poverty, but not climate change.

This deprioritization of climate refugees in relation to more "pressing" instances of forced migration ignores the unique (and, at present, insuperable) challenges that they face. It also fails to recognise the evidence that the climate is responsible, in part, for the crises that we in the West are more "familiar" with. At the least, as researchers argue—and the UNHCR acknowledges—environmental change frequently "makes a bad situation worse." Many have suggested reasons for the bias, including: climate refugees' lack of official status, diverging interests in the global North and South, debates over labelling someone a "climate refugee," falling news coverage of climate issues, and the fact that those who presently suffer most are people of colour. Whatever the cause, our reluctance to grapple with the needs and narratives of climate refugees places the political, financial, and technological resources of the international community increasingly out of reach.

The lack of international support has forced small island states to make their own resettlement arrangements, often at the cost of their self-determination and cultural heritage. Kiribati has recently bought a small piece of land in Fiji to house its some 100,000 citizens when its own land becomes uninhabitable. The Maldives have a similar plan with the creation of a "sovereign wealth fund" in order to purchase patches of land in Sri Lanka or India; Indonesia has also offered to "rent" some of its 17,000 islands to displaced communities. Other, less conventional solutions are also being explored: French Polynesia has just this week signed a deal with the Seasteading Institute to develop Floating Islands, or "self floating environments." While such solutions may address the problem in the short-term, they pale in comparison to longer-term protections that we usually afford to more "conventional" refugees. In expecting climate refugees to remedy their own displacement, we fail not only to meet our humanitarian obligations, but also to take responsibility for the most hard-hitting effects of climate change.

Different and more equitable solutions are possible for climate refugees only with the support and cooperation of the international community. This is why, in speaking up against Trump's policies on climate change, we must focus on amplifying the voices of those who are the most affected. Climate refugees are already struggling to be heard. We must do our best to listen.

Periodical and Internet Sources Bibliography

The following articles have been selected to supplement the diverse views presented in this chapter.

John Abraham, "Reflections on the politics of climate change." *Guardian*, June 2, 2017. https://www.theguardian.com/ environment/climate-consensus-97-per-cent/2017/jun/02/ reflections-on-the-politics-of-climate-change

Ron Brownstein, "A political blockade is colliding with the evidence on climate change." CNN Politics, November 27, 2018. https:// www.cnn.com/2018/11/27/politics/brown-blockade-climate- change/index.html

Sarah Childress, "Timeline: The Politics of Climate Change." Frontline, October 23, 2012. https://www.pbs.org/wgbh/frontline/ article/timeline-the-politics-of-climate-change/

Coral Davenport and Eric Lipton, "How G.O.P. Leaders Came to View Climate Change as Fake Science." *New York Times*, June 3, 2017. https://www.nytimes.com/2017/06/03/us/politics/ republican-leaders-climate-change.html

David Doniger, "Climate Change Is Changing the Politics of Climate Change." NRDC, November 26, 2018. https://www.nrdc.org/ experts/david-doniger/climate-change-changing-politics-climate- change

Clare Foran, "Donald Trump and the Triumph of Climate-Change Denial." *Atlantic*, December 25, 2016. https://www.theatlantic. com/politics/archive/2016/12/donald-trump-climate-change- skeptic-denial/510359/

Cary Funk and Brian Kennedy, "The Politics of Climate." Pew Research Center, October 4, 2016. http://www.pewinternet. org/2016/10/04/the-politics-of-climate/

David Manuel-Navarrete, "Climate change and power: Isn't it all about politics?" Kings College, London, 2010. https://www.kcl. ac.uk/sspp/departments/geography/research/research-domains/ contested-development/manuel-navarettewp32.pdf

Manjana Milkoreit, "Imaginary politics: Climate change and making the future." Element A Science, 2018. https://www.elementascience.org/articles/10.1525/elementa.249/print/

Daniel Ryan, "Politics And Climate Change: Exploring The Relationship Between Political Parties And Climate Issues In Latin America." SciElo. http://www.scielo.br/scielo.php?script=sci_arttext&pid=S1414-753X2017000300271

Robin Shear, "Politics of (Climate) Change." University of Miami, 2018. http://climate.miami.edu/politics-of-climate-change/

GLOBAL VIEWPOINTS

CHAPTER 4

| An Uneasy Future

In Tuvalu and Kiribati Residents Must Find New Homes When the Islands Become Submerged

Rana Balesh

The International Panel on Climate Change has recognized that climate change will significantly impact the world, especially vulnerable places and their populations. Small island developing states (SIDS) such as Tuvalu and Kiribati are already being impacted. In the following excerpted viewpoint, Rana Balesh presents case studies on these two island nations and what needs to be done to address their situations. The studies particularly address the potential plight of climate refugees from these areas. Balesh received her juris doctor from Florida A&M University in 2014.

As you read, consider the following questions:

1. What did the IPCC define as the cause of climate change?
2. Why are SIDS especially vulnerable to the effects of climate change?
3. Why are indigenous people so greatly affected by leaving their homes?

The effects of global climate change are being felt around the world.[1] The U.N. Human Rights Council has recognized that climate change will significantly impact vulnerable

"Submerging Islands: Tuvalu and Kiribati as Case Studies Illustrating the Need for a Climate Refugee Treaty," by Rana Balesh, Florida A&M University College of Law, 2015.

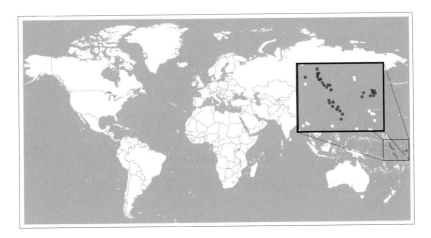

populations.[2] The Intergovernmental Panel on Climate Change (IPCC) has confirmed that anthropogenic sources affect climate change.[3] Research has shown that climate change is caused in part through human activities that cause the release of greenhouse gas emissions (GHGs).[4] GHGs mainly come from the burning of fossil fuels.[5] When GHGs become trapped in the atmosphere, they cause the Earth to warm.[6] The Earth's temperature has risen due to the additional GHGs in the atmosphere.[7] The effects of climate change cannot be ignored.[8]

Climate change has impacted the environment in many different ways such as affecting the amount of rainfall per year and causing changes to agriculture and forests.[9] Climate change has also caused a rise in sea levels.[10] As a consequence of sea level rise, many island states are experiencing coastal erosion.[11]

Small island developing states (SIDS) are particularly vulnerable to the rise in sea level due to low elevations.[12] The loss of territory is not the only concern for SIDS as infrastructure and food sources are also at risk.[13] Unfortunately, many SIDS do not have the financial and technological resources to effectively handle these issues.[14] Many SIDS are in danger of complete submersion.[15]

Many island indigenous peoples are connected to the land as it provides them both their identity and livelihood.[16] The loss of land for indigenous peoples also means a loss of identity.[17] Many island nations will soon succumb to rising sea levels, causing indigenous populations to be without homes; therefore, effective action must be taken soon.[18]

Tuvalu and Kiribati are examples of states in the Pacific Ocean that are being affected by climate change.[19] They are both projected to disappear by 2050.[20] SIDS, such as Tuvalu and Kiribati, are utilizing adaptation and mitigation strategies to cope with the effects of climate change.[21] The process of adaptation, as it is related to environmental issues, refers to people's ability to adjust to changes caused by climate change.[22] Adaptation measures include creating new ways to harvest crops, water storage, relocating inland from the coast, and changing governmental policies on climate change.[23] Some states have formed national adaptation programmes of action (NAPAs), which identify and prioritize adaptation needs.[24] Both Tuvalu[25] and Kiribati[26] have implemented NAPAs. Adaptation measures will not help some island nations in the long term because total submersion into the ocean is inevitable.[27]

In 2009, it was estimated that there are twenty-five to thirty million environmentally displaced persons also known as climate change refugees.[28] This number is expected to increase to approximately 200 million by 2050.[29] Climate refugees were first recognized in 1987 when it was determined that many people were going to have to leave their homes in their native countries due to environmental factors.[30] Citizens of Tuvalu and Kiribati will have to leave their native countries because the islands on which they reside are at risk of submersion.[31]

Although there is a growing recognition that climate displacement is occurring, there is no comprehensive legal framework in place that currently protects climate refugees.[32] Unfortunately, there is no legal instrument in existence under international law that provides climate refugees the rights and protections they need for survival.[33]

[…]

I. The Plight of Climate Refugees

A. Climate Change Impacts

Climate is changing and Earth's temperature is increasing.[34] According to the Environmental Protection Agency (EPA), the Earth's temperature has increased 1.4°F in the last century, and it is estimated that it will rise an additional 2°F to 11.5°F in the next century.[35]

Climate change is causing a rise in sea level.[36] Rises in sea level occur when the mass or volume of water increases in the Earth's oceans.[37]

[...]

There are conflicting projections on how much the sea level will rise in the future.[44] The Fifth Assessment Report of the Intergovernmental Panel on Climate Change (IPCC) has projected that sea level will rise between .17m and .82m by 2100.[45] However, another study has indicated that sea level will rise between 75cm and 190cm by 2100 when taking into consideration the melting of polar ice sheets.[46]

The rise in sea level has impacted the environment in many different ways.[47] Studies have proven that rising sea levels create a higher flood risk, causing coastal erosion and salt-water intrusion into ground water.[48] These impacts can threaten the island populations by destroying food sources such as crops and access to fresh water.[49] Rise in sea level is also causing the degradation of coastal ecosystems, which has a direct effect on island indigenous populations since their survival is connected to the land on which they reside.[50]

B. Small Island Developing States

SIDS are especially vulnerable to the effects of climate change due to the locations.[51] Climate change has impacted SIDS in many different ways such as altering the weather by increasing storms like cyclones and hurricanes.[52] These types of weather events can cause damage to crops and fisheries that not only affect the local economy, but also the indigenous peoples' livelihood as well.[53] SIDS are vulnerable to rising sea levels as it increases shoreline erosion, which in turn places island states at risk of losing their homes and infrastructure.[54] Many SIDS are at risk of becoming uninhabitable.[55] High population densities and limited financial resources make it difficult for islands to take effective action against the effects of climate change.[56]

Rising sea levels are causing islands to become completely submerged by the ocean.[57] Consequently, many island nations are at risk of losing their territory.[58] Island nations have taken adaptation measures to combat this risk of their territories becoming uninhabitable.[59] Scholars have suggested that island nations use both hard and soft protection measures to protect against rising sea levels.[60] For example, a hard protection measure could include the building of a seawall, whereas a soft protection measure could include artificial elevation of an island.[61] The implementation of these measures can be very problematic, however, especially in terms of cost as they are very expensive.[62] For example, it will cost the Marshall Islands $100 million dollars to construct a sea wall.[63] Migration is another adaptation measure.[64] Under this measure, people may migrate out of their home countries, or within their country, which is internal migration.[65] Since 1987, the issues surrounding climate refugees have been brought to the public's attention with increasing regularity.[66]

C. Case Studies in Prospective Climate Refugees
1. Tuvalu

Tuvalu is located in the Pacific Ocean between Hawaii and Australia.[67] Tuvalu is less than 2 meters above sea level and consists of nine islands.[68] The name, Tuvalu, actually means "eight islands together."[69] Tuvalu's total area is 26 square kilometers and ranks as the fourth smallest country in the world.[70] It has approximately 10,000 citizens.[71] Its primary source of living is through fishing and farming.[72] Tuvaluans are connected to their land.[73] Their land represents not only their home, but also their identity.[74] They live by the maxim, "land is life, without land there is no life."[75] This connection between the people of Tuvalu and their land means that the effects of climate change will not only mean a loss of territory, but also a loss in cultural and social identity.[76] Tuvaluans have contributed very little to GHG emissions that cause climate change.[77]

Yet, Tuvalu is profoundly affected by climate change.[78] Flooding is a serious issue that has caused massive destruction to homes.[79] It has also caused saltwater contamination in inland soil and has resulted in the death of coconut trees.[80] In addition, drought has resulted in limiting the supply of water.[81] Tuvalu can desalinate the seawater, but it is too expensive for Tuvalu to pursue by itself.[82] In 2011, fresh water was in such short supply that it caused local schools and hospitals to shut down.[83] New Zealand and Australia had to provide aid to Tuvalu during that period.[84]

Shoreline erosion has caused a loss of farming land and a loss in income.[85] Farming in the inner part of the island has been affected negatively because of the high level of salt in the soil and groundwater.[86] In addition, there are concerns that the number of Tuvaluans that suffer from illness and disease will increase in the future because of the lack of drinking water and adequate food production in that country.[87]

Tuvalu is projected to disappear by 2050.[88] In 2000, the Tuvaluan government asked Australia and New Zealand to accept their citizens as refugees.[89] However, Australia is not accepting climate refugees at this time, and New Zealand only accepts 75 citizens every year between the ages of 18-45 through its labor migration program.[90] New Zealand's policies regarding climate change refugees are insufficient.[91] By 2050, New Zealand will have only accepted 2,275 of Tuvalu's 10,000 citizens.[92] Furthermore, that does not include the number of Tuvaluans that do not meet the requirements of New Zealand's labor migration program.[93] Therefore, New Zealand's labor migration program is not an effective solution to climate displacement and other more effective proposals need to be considered.[94]

In 2002, Tuvalu announced that it was considering a possible suit against the United States and Australia in the International Court of Justice (ICJ) over the negative effects of climate change stating that these two countries are the most liable for releasing GHGs that are contributing to climate change.[95] However, Tuvalu will most likely find it difficult to litigate this issue, as there are numerous issues with such a case before the ICJ.[96] For instance, the United States has not accepted compulsory jurisdiction under the ICJ.[97] If jurisdiction is established, Tuvalu will have difficulty proving breach and causation.[98] For example, Tuvalu will have to prove that Australia and the US had an obligation under the Kyoto Protocol to reduce emissions, but since it failed to do so it has caused Tuvalu to suffer effects from climate change.[99] Tuvalu will have to resolve complex issues to bring a suit against the United States and Australia in front of the ICJ.[100]

In 2009, the Tuvaluan Prime Minister Apisai Ielemia stated that Tuvalu was not considering migration as a solution to their submerging islands.[101] He stated,

> "[W]hile Tuvalu faces an uncertain future because of climate change . . . it is our view that Tuvaluans will remain in Tuvalu. We will fight to keep our country, our culture and our way of living. We are not considering any migration scheme. We believe if the right actions are taken to address climate change, Tuvalu will survive."[102]

However, without an adequate legal framework to address climate change, Tuvalu will not survive.[103]

[...]

Notes

1. See Mary-Elena Carr, Madeleine Rubenstein, Alice Graff & Diego Villareal, "Sea Level Rise in a Changing Climate," in *Threatened Island Nations* 15 (Michael B. Gerrard & Gregory E. Wannier eds., 2013).

2. See U.N. Human Rights Council Res. 10/4, U.N. Doc. A/HRC/RES/10/4 (Mar. 25, 2009), available at http://ap.ohchr.org/documents/E/HRC/resolutions/A_HRC_RES_10_4.pdf.

3. Samadu Atapattu, "Climate Change, Human Rights and Forced Migration: Implications for International Law," 27 *Wis. Int'l L.J.* 607 (2009).

4. Intergovernmental Panel on Climate Change 4th Assessment Report, Synthesis Report: Summary for Policymakers," at 6, available at http://www.ipcc.ch/pdf/assessment-report/ar4/syr/ar4_syr_spm.pdf (discussing that GHG emissions will continue to increase in the future).

5. "Causes of Climate Change," EPA, http://www.epa.gov/climatechange/science/causes. html (last visited Nov. 9, 2013).

6. Id.

7. Id.

8. See, e.g., Atapattu, supra note 3, at 608 (discussing the impact of climate change on forced migration).

9. "Climate Change Impacts and Adopting to Change," EPA, http://www.epa.gov/climatechange/impacts-adaptation/ (last visited Dec. 30, 2013).

10. See "Coastal Areas: Climate Impacts on Coastal Areas," EPA, http://www.epa.gov/climatechange/impacts-adaptation/coasts.html (last visited Dec. 30, 2012).

11. Mary-Elena Carr et al., supra note 1, at 40.

12. Id.

13. "Saving Paradise: Ensuring Sustainable Development," WMO (Dec. 30, 2012), available at http://www.wmo.int/pages/publications/showcase/documents/WMO973.pdf [hereinafter Saving Paradise].

14. Ana Weinbaum, "Unjust Enrichment: An Alternative to Tort Law and Human Rights in the Climate Change Context," 20 *Pac. Rim. L. & Pol'y J.* 429, 430, 431 (2011).

15. Saving Paradise, supra note 13.

16. Keely Boom, "The Rising Tide of International Climate Litigation: An Illustrative hypothetical of Tuvalu v. Australia," in *Climate Change and Indigenous Peoples: The Search for Legal Remedies*, 409, 411 (Randall S. Abate & Elizabeth Ann Kronk eds., 2013).

17. Id.

18. See Jane McAdam, "Swimming Against the Tide: Why a Climate Change Displacement Treaty is Not the Answer," 23 *Int'l J. of Refugee L.*, 2, 8 (2011), available at http://papers.ssrn.com/sol3/papers.cfm?abstract_id=1714714.

19. "Our Pacific Neighbours on the Frontline," *Oxfam Australia*, https://www.oxfam.org.au/explore/climate-change/impacts-of-climate-change/ourpacific-neighbours-on-the-frontline/ (last visited Nov. 7, 2013).

20. McAdam, supra note 18, at 8.

21. See Ryan Jarvis, "Sinking Nations and Climate Change Adaptation Strategies," 9 *Seattle J. for Soc. Just.* 447, 460 (2010). A discussion of climate change mitigation is outside the scope of this paper.

22. Id.

23. "Vulnerability and Adaptation to Climate Change in Small Island Developing States," *Climate Change Secretariat*, 72 and 83, available at https://unfccc.int/files/adaptation/adverse_effects_and_response_measures_art_48/appli cation/pdf/2007 02_sids_adaptation_bg.pdf.

24. Id.

25. "Tuvalu's National Adaptation Programme of Action," *Ministry of Natural Resources, Environment, Agriculture and Lands* 22 (2007), available at http://unfccc.int/resource/docs/napa/tuv01.pdf.

26. Government of Kiribati, "Republic of Kiribati National Adaptation Program of Action (NAPA)," 1 (2007), available at http://unfccc.int/resource/docs/napa/kir01.pdf.

27. McAdam, supra note 18, at 8.

28. Atapattu, supra note 3, at 610.

29. Id. at 611.

30. Id.

31. See Jenny G. Stoutenburg, "When Do States Disappear? Thresholds of Effective Statehood and the Continued Recognition of 'Deterritorialized' Island States," *Threatened Island Nations* 57, 58 (Michael B. Gerrard & Gregory E. Wannier eds., 2013).

32. Jeremy Kelley, "Climate Change and Small Island States: Adrift in a Raising Sea of Legal Uncertainty," 11 *Sustainable Dev. L & Pol'y*, no. 2, 56, (2011), available at http://digitalcommons.wcl.american.edu/cgi/ viewcontent.cgi?article=1474&context=sdlp.

33. See id.

34. "Climate Change: Basic Information," EPA, http://www.epa.gov/climatechange/basics/ (last visited Nov. 8, 2013). [hereinafter EPA].

35. Id.

36. Mary Elena-Carr et al., supra note 1, at 15.

37. Id.

44. Id. at 32.

45. Intergovernmental Panel on Climate Change 5th Assessment Report, Climate Change 2013: Summary for Policymakers, at 21, available at. http://www.ipcc.ch/pdf/assessment-report/ar5/wg1/WG1AR5_SPM_FINAL.pdf

46. Martin Vermeer & Stefan Rahmstorf, "Global Seal Level Linked to Global Temperature," 106 *Proceedings of the Nat'l Acad. Sci.* 21527, 21530 (2009).

47. Mostafa Naser, "Climate Change, Environmental Degradation, and Migration: A Complex Nexus," 36 *Wm. & Mary Envtl. Pol'y Rev.* 713, 724 (2012), available at http://scholarship.law.wm.edu/cgi/viewcontent.cgi?article=1550&context=wmelpr.

48. Mary-Elena Carr et al., supra note 1, at 42.

49. Naser, supra note 47, at 724.

50. See Mary-Elena Carr et al., supra note 1, at 42.

51. See id. at 41.

52. "Climate Change: Small Island Developing States," *Climate Change Secretariat* (2005), available at http://www.unfccc.int/resource/docs/publications/cc_sids.pdf.

53. "The Impact of Climate Change on the Development Prospects of the Least Developed Countries and Small Island Developing States," *UN-Ohrlls* 29–30 (2009), available at http://www.unohrlls.org/UserFiles/File/LDC%20Documents /The%20impact%20 of%20CC%20on%20LDCs%20and%20SIDS%20for%20web.pdf.

54. Mary-Elena Carr et al., supra note 1, at 43.

55. See, e.g., Stoutenburg, supra note 31, at 57 (arguing that a State can still exist under international law even when they no longer meet the traditional requirements of statehood).

56. Naser, supra note 47, at 724.

57. Kelley, supra note 32, at 56.

58. Id.

59. Stoutenburg, supra note 31, at 62 (stating that SIDS should use protection measures to keep from submerging completely into the ocean).

60. Id.

61. Id.

62. Erika J. Techera, "Climate Change, Legal Governance and the Pacific Islands," *Climate Change and Indigenous Peoples: The Search for Legal Remedies*, 339, 351 (Randall S. Abate & Elizabeth Ann Kronk eds., 2013).

63. See id. at 615.

64. Attapattu, supra note 3, at 613.

65. Id.

66. See id. at 610.

67. World Factbook: Tuvalu, CIA, https://www.cia.gov/library/publications/theworld-factbook/geos/tv.html (last visited Nov. 17, 2013).

68. Boom, supra note 16, at 410.

69. See, e.g., About Tuvalu, http://www.tuvaluislands.com/about.htm (last visited Nov. 10, 2013).

70. Id.

71. Boom, supra note 16, at 410.

72. Id.

73. Id. at 411.

74. Id.

75. Id.

76. Id.

77. Id. at 410.

78. Amelia H. Krales, "As Danger Laps at Its Shores, Tuvalu Pleads for Action," *Green Blog* (Oct. 18, 2011, 5:00 AM), http://green.blogs.nytimes.com/2011/10/18/as-danger-laps-at-its-shores-tuvalu-pleadsfor-action/?_r=0 (Tuvaluan business owner stated, "I have been to the islets to get some coconuts from a piece of land there and three-quarters had been taken away by the sea" [hereinafter Tuvalu Pleads].

79. Id.

80. "Tuvalu's Views on Possible Security Implications," U.N. Secretary General (2009), available at http://www.un.org/esa/dsd/resources/res_pdfs/ga-64/ccinputs/Tuvalu_CCIS.pdf [hereinafter Tuvalu's Views].

81. See id.

82. Id.

83. See "Australia, New Zealand in a Airlift to Drought-Hit Tuvalu," BBC News AsiaPacific (Oct. 7, 2011, 3:15 AM), http://www.bbc.co.uk/news/world-asia-pacific15210568.

84. "Australia, New Zealand in a Airlift to Drought-Hit Tuvalu," BBC News AsiaPacific (Oct. 7, 2011, 3:15 AM), http://www.bbc.co.uk/news/world-asia-pacific15210568. Id.

85. Krales, supra note 78.

86. Id.

87. Tuvalu's Views, supra note 80.

88. McAdam, supra note 18, at 8.

89. World Factbook: Tuvalu, supra note 67.

90. Atapattu supra note 3, at 633.

91. Id.

92. See id.

93. See id.

94. See id.

95. Boom, supra note 16, at 412; See also "Tiny Pacific Nation Takes on Australia," BBC News (Mar. 4, 2002), http://news.bbc.co.uk/2/hi/asia-pacific/1854118.stm.

96. Id. at 417–32

97. Id. at 421.

98. Id. at 417–32.

99. Id. at 427, 433.

100. Id. at 417–32.

101. "Only if the Right Actions are Taken Will We Survive—Tuvalu PM Issues Call to Save His Country From Extinction," *La Treizieme Étoile* (Dec. 10, 2009), http://www. andrewjburgesseu.blogspot.com/2009_12_06_archive.html (meetings took place at the Parliament's Committee on Development).

102. Id.

103. See Bonnie Docherty & Tyler Giannini, "Confronting a Rising Tide: A Proposal for a Climate Refugee Treaty," 33 *Harv. Envtl. L. Rev.* 349, 357 (2009).

Nations Should Prepare Now to Help the Millions Who Will Be Displaced by Climate Change

Gulrez Shah Azhar

Climate change will force millions of people to become climate refugees in the coming decades. In the following viewpoint Gulrez Shah Azhar underlines the need to enact policies and actions on the regional, national, and global level, both short term and long term, to deal with this impending level of migration. Included in that is the need to recognize the status of climate refugees, on the same level as the refugee status given to political and disaster refugees. Azhar is a doctoral candidate at the Pardee RAND Graduate School and an Assistant Policy Researcher at the RAND Corporation in Santa Monica.

As you read, consider the following questions:

1. What are some of the things that the author feels must take place on the national, regional, and global level concerning climate migrants?
2. Why is it important to recognize climate refugees as having the same status as political or disaster refugees?
3. What short-term steps does the author recommend to the global community concerning climate refugees?

"Climate change will displace millions in coming decades. Nations should prepare now to help them," by Gulrez Shah Azhar, The Conversation, 12/19/2017. https://theconversation.com/climate-change-will-displace-millions-in-coming-decades-nations-should-prepare-now-to-help-them-89274. Licenced under CC BY-ND 4.0.

W ildfires tearing across Southern California have forced thousands of residents to evacuate from their homes. Even more people fled ahead of the hurricanes that slammed into Texas and Florida earlier this year, jamming highways and filling hotels. A viral social media post showed a flight-radar picture of people trying to escape Florida and posed a provocative question: What if the adjoining states were countries and didn't grant escaping migrants refuge?

By the middle of this century, experts estimate that climate change is likely to displace between 150 and 300 million people. If this group formed a country, it would be the fourth-largest in the world, with a population nearly as large as that of the United States.

Yet neither individual countries nor the global community are completely prepared to support a whole new class of "climate migrants." As a physician and public health researcher in India, I learned the value of surveillance and early warning systems for managing infectious disease outbreaks. Based on my current research on health impacts of heat waves in developing countries, I believe much needs to be done at the national, regional and global level to deal with climate migrants.

Millions Displaced Yearly

Climate migration is already happening. Every year desertification in Mexico's drylands forces 700,000 people to relocate. Cyclones have displaced thousands from Tuvalu in the South Pacific and Puerto Rico in the Caribbean. Experts agree that a prolonged drought may have catalyzed Syria's civil war and resulting migration.

Between 2008 and 2015, an average of 26.4 million people per year were displaced by climate- or weather-related disasters, according to the United Nations. And the science of climate change indicates that these trends are likely to get worse. With each one-degree increase in temperature, the air's moisture-carrying capacity increases by 7 percent, fueling increasingly severe storms. Sea levels may rise by as much as three feet by the year 2100, submerging coastal areas and inhabited islands.

50,000 Climate Migrants Could Flee the Coasts for Denver

Rising seas and violent storms could devastate the American coasts, wrecking Southern economies and driving hundreds of thousands of people inland toward cities like Denver, Chicago and Austin. That's the grim prognosis of a pair of recent studies that aim to measure the human impact of climate change in the United States.

Taken together, these studies put the High Plains right in the middle of the pack when it comes to climate vulnerability, facing both direct concerns and the indirect consequences of damage to other areas.

Basically, we're protected from rising seas and the worst weather—but Colorado could face a lot of its own problems. "The climate models have greater extremes for the South. It pops up for a lot of the Gulf area: much more extreme storms, more potential for bigger events," said Paul Chinowsky, professor of sustainable development at CU Boulder and co-founder of Resilient Analytics.

In contrast, in Colorado, "we get a little more gradual change. It's just a consistent raising of temperatures." Still, that comes with big implications, according to Chinowsky. "Colorado really doesn't have, historically, the structures and environmental health concerns for high temperatures," he said.

That's part of the reason that the city of Denver has started research to see which neighborhoods and people might be most affected by the expected 100-degree summers. Colorado also might have broader implications. Wildfire season has grown consistently longer here over recent decades; a Columbia University study linked climate change to increased fire in the West. In a state where cities so often cluster against the wilderness frontier, that can be a major economic concern.

There's also the question of water and drought. A recent study with a Colorado State University author found that about a third of the 17-year decline in the Colorado River's flows could be attributed to higher temperatures and climate change. Damage to ecosystems, water supplies and the national economy still could hurt the Mountain West and its economy. It all adds up to a bigger question: Even if it dodges the most serious impacts of climate change, will Colorado have the resources to accept those who are less fortunate?

"50,000 climate migrants could flee the coasts for Denver, studies say, but Colorado's threats are serious too," by Andrew Kenney, Spirited Media, July 5, 2017.

The Pacific islands are extremely vulnerable, as are more than 410 US cities and others around the globe, including Amsterdam, Hamburg, Lisbon and Mumbai. Rising temperatures could make parts of west Asia inhospitable to human life. On the same day that Hurricane Irma roared over Florida in September, heavy rains on the other side of the world submerged one-third of Bangladesh and eastern parts of India, killing thousands.

Climate change will affect most everyone on the planet to some degree, but poor people in developing nations will be affected most severely. Extreme weather events and tropical diseases wreak the heaviest damage in these regions. Undernourished people who have few resources and inadequate housing are especially at risk and likely to be displaced.

Recognize and Plan for Climate Migrants Now

Today the global community has not universally acknowledged the existence of climate migrants, much less agreed on how to define them. According to international refugee law, climate migrants are not legally considered refugees. Therefore, they have none of the protections officially accorded to refugees, who are technically defined as people fleeing persecution. No global agreements exist to help millions of people who are displaced by natural disasters every year.

Refugees' rights, and nations' legal obligation to defend them, were first defined under the 1951 Refugee Convention, which was expanded in 1967. This work took place well before it was apparent that climate change would become a major force driving migrations and creating refugee crises.

Under the convention, a refugee is defined as someone "unable or unwilling to return to their country of origin owing to a well-founded fear of being persecuted for reasons of race, religion, nationality, membership of a particular social group, or political opinion." The convention legally binds nations to provide access to courts, identity papers and travel documents, and to offer possible naturalization. It also bars discriminating against refugees, penalizing them, expelling them or forcibly returning them to their countries of origin. Refugees are entitled to practice their religions, attain education and access public assistance.

In my view, governments and organizations such as the United Nations should consider modifying international law to provide legal status to environmental refugees and establish protections and rights for them. Reforms could factor in the concept of "climate justice," the notion that climate change is an ethical and social concern. After all, richer countries have contributed the most to cause warming, while poor countries will bear the most disastrous consequences.

Some observers have suggested that countries that bear major responsibility for greenhouse gas emissions should take in more refugees. Alternatively, the world's largest carbon polluters could contribute to a fund that would pay for refugee care and resettlement for those temporarily and permanently displaced.

The Paris climate agreement does not mention climate refugees. However, there have been some consultations and initiatives by various organizations and governments. They include efforts to create a climate change displacement coordination facility and a U.N. Special Rapporteur on Human Rights and Climate Change.

It is tough to define a climate refugee or migrant. This could be one of the biggest challenges in developing policies.

As history has shown, destination countries respond to waves of migration in various ways, ranging from welcoming immigrants to placing them in detention camps or denying them assistance. Some countries may be selective in whom they allow in, favoring only the young and productive while leaving children, the elderly and infirm behind. A guiding global policy could help prevent confusion and outline some minimum standards.

Short-term Actions

Negotiating international agreements on these issues could take many years. For now, major G20 powers such as the United States, the European Union, China, Russia, India, Canada,

Australia and Brazil should consider intermediate steps. The United States could offer temporary protected status to climate migrants who are already on its soil. Government aid programs and nongovernment organizations should ramp up support to refugee relief organizations and ensure that aid reaches refugees from climate disasters.

In addition, all countries that have not signed the United Nations refugee conventions could consider joining them. This includes many developing countries in South Asia and the Middle East that are highly vulnerable to climate change and that already have large refugee populations. Since most of the affected people in these countries will likely move to neighboring nations, it is crucial that all countries in these regions abide by a common set of policies for handling and assisting refugees.

The scale of this challenge is unlike anything humanity has ever faced. By midcentury, climate change is likely to uproot far more people than World War II, which displaced some 60 million across Europe, or the Partition of India, which affected approximately 15 million. The migration crisis that has gripped Europe since 2015 has involved something over one million refugees and migrants. It is daunting to envision much larger flows of people, but that is why the global community should start doing so now.

In the United Arab Emirates, Qatar, Saudi Arabia, and Iran, Extreme Heatwaves Could Push the Climate Beyond Human Endurance

Damian Carrington

In the following viewpoint Damian Carrington presents research to show that the Middle East may soon be suffering heat waves of such intensity that human survival will no longer be possible there. He also presents some of the reasons why the Middle East is forecasted to become a hotspot, and some of the methods used to measure the intensity of heat and humidity. Personal accounts of what it is like to live in such hot temperatures are also included, and how the heat is a huge risk for religious worshippers in Mecca and Jeddah. Carrington is Environment editor for the Guardian.

As you read, consider the following questions:

1. Why is the Gulf in the Middle East forecasted to be a global hotspot?
2. What is wet bulb temperature? Why is it important in researching heat waves?
3. Why are the heat levels at Mecca and Jeddah especially worrying?

"Extreme heatwaves could push Gulf climate beyond human endurance, study shows," by Damian Carrington, Guardian News and Media Limited, October 26, 2015. Reprinted by permission.

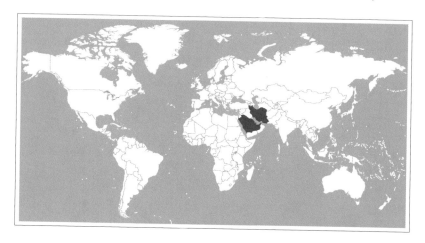

The Gulf in the Middle East, the heartland of the global oil industry, will suffer heatwaves beyond the limit of human survival if climate change is unchecked, according to a new scientific study.

The extreme heatwaves will affect Abu Dhabi, Dubai, Doha and coastal cities in Iran as well as posing a deadly threat to millions of Hajj pilgrims in Saudi Arabia, when the religious festival falls in the summer. The study shows the extreme heatwaves, more intense than anything ever experienced on Earth, would kick in after 2070 and that the hottest days of today would by then be a near-daily occurrence.

"Our results expose a specific regional hotspot where climate change, in the absence of significant [carbon cuts], is likely to severely impact human habitability in the future," said Prof Jeremy Pal and Prof Elfatih Eltahir, both at the Massachusetts Institute of Technology, writing in the journal *Nature Climate Change*.

They said the future climate for many locations in the Gulf would be like today's extreme climate in the desert of Northern Afar, on the African side of the Red Sea, where there are no permanent human settlements at all. But the research also showed that cutting greenhouse gas emissions now could avoid this fate.

Oil and gas rich nations in the region, particularly Saudi Arabia, have frequently tried to frustrate international climate change negotiations. The Gulf, where populations are rising quickly, was hit in 2015 by one of its worst-ever heatwaves, where temperatures topped 50C (122F) and led to a significant number of deaths.

Prof Eltahir said: "We would hope that information like this would be helpful in making sure there is interest [in cutting carbon emissions] for the countries in the region. They have a vital interest in supporting measures that would help reduce the concentration of CO2 in the future."

The new research examined how a combined measure of temperature and humidity, called wet bulb temperature (WBT), would increase if carbon emissions continue on current trends and the world warms by 4C this century.

At WBTs above 35C, the high heat and humidity make it physically impossible for even the fittest human body to cool itself by sweating, with fatal consequences after six hours. For less fit people, the fatal WBT is below 35C. A WBT temperature of 35C—the combination of 46C heat and 50% humidity—was almost reached in Bandar Mahshahr in Iran in July 2015.

The scientists used standard climate computer models to show that the fatal WBT extremes would occur every decade or two after 2070 along most of the Gulf coast, if global warming is not curbed. Using the normal measure of temperature, the study shows 45C would become the usual summer maximum in Gulf cities, with 60C being seen in places like Kuwait City in some years.

Near the Red Sea coast of Saudi Arabia, where Mecca and Jeddah lie, the WBT is not projected to pass the fatal 35C level, but would be 32C or 33C. This would make the Hajj extremely hazardous, said the scientists. "One of the rituals of Hajj—the day of Arafah—involves worshipping at the site outside Mecca from sunrise to sunset. In these kind of conditions, it would be very hard to have outside rituals," said Eltahir.

Air conditioning might be able to protect people indoors and those in wealthy Gulf oil states might be able to afford it, said the scientists, but less wealthy nations would suffer. In Yemen, for example, the WBT would reach 33C. "Under such conditions, climate change would possibly lead to premature death of the weakest—namely children and the elderly," they said.

However, global action to cut carbon emissions would mean the fatal WBT would not be passed and that temperatures in Saudi Arabia would experience much smaller rises. "The [Gulf] countries stand to gain considerable benefits by supporting the global efforts" to cut emissions, said the scientists.

"The consequences of major heatwaves for human health has become apparent from the death toll of recent events such as those in Chicago in 1995, Europe in 2003 [30,000 deaths] and Russia in 2010 [50,000 deaths]," said climate scientist Prof Christoph Schär, at ETH Zurich, Switzerland and who was not involved in the study. But he said the new study "concerns another category of heat waves—one that may be fatal to everybody affected, even young and fit individuals under shaded and well-ventilated outdoor conditions."

Schär said the work showed the threat to human health from climate change may be much more severe, and occur much earlier, than previously thought. "It also indicates that reducing global greenhouse gas emissions and adaptation efforts are essential for the inhabitants of the Gulf and Red Sea regions."

The Gulf is vulnerable to very high WBT because regional weather patterns mean it has clear summer skies, allowing the sun to strongly warm the waters of the Gulf, which are shallow and therefore heat up more than deeper oceans. This heating of the sea also produces high humidity, meaning cities near the coast are most affected.

What's It Like Living in Today's Gulf Heatwaves

Growing up in Dubai in the Gulf, the thing I looked forward to the most every summer was leaving.

Summer meant going back to my birthplace in Alexandria in Egypt, but it also meant getting away from temperatures that could hit a hellish 50C, when going to the beach wasn't an option, unless you enjoyed scorching your soles in the sand to swim in tepid seawater while burning your skin in the blazing sun.

Summer is something you work around in the Gulf. You try to ensure your time spent outside is kept to a minimum because the high humidity of seaside cities, such as Dubai, will leave your clothes soaking wet within minutes. It means an intricate hop from air-conditioned site to air-conditioned site—your apartment to your car to the supermarket or the shopping mall or a friend's similarly temperature-controlled abode. It means never having to use a water heater because your shower will always be hot—even scaldingly so if you dare to take one at midday.

Now that the holy month of Ramadan falls in the summer, whenever I'm back visiting family I try to keep daytime waking hours, when I have to abstain from drinking water, to a bare minimum. I've completed the hajj and the lesser pilgrimage, the umra—the former in the cool February climate and the latter in the heat of summer. I cannot imagine handling the crush of millions of pilgrims marching around the ka'aba in the Grand Mosque during a heatwave.

The summer can be insufferable in other places in the region for different reasons. While this year it was relatively mild in Beirut, where I live now, for example, it is always accompanied by water shortages and extended power cuts for days on end, leaving you with little choice but to pay for an expensive generator subscription to preserve perishables such as meat or dairy for more than a day, or sleeping on the ceramic tiles to cool off. This year it was also accompanied by piles of rotting trash baking in the sun after the government's chronic failures were extended to garbage collection.

This isn't a problem in the Gulf, where save for a freak power cut the constant electricity supply maintains a climate-controlled habitat. I was a bit incredulous when Qatar was awarded the World Cup hosting rights—I hadn't been able to play football outside of an air-conditioned indoor pitch in the summer since God knows how long.

Oppressive Humidity Will Make Certain Parts of the World Uninhabitable

Kevin Krajick

In the following viewpoint Kevin Krajick discusses the role of humidity in heat waves, and why it is a major factor in places that are warming due to climate change. Climate scientists are already forecasting that killer heat waves will become increasingly common as the world's climate warms, but many studies have not addressed the role of humidity and how it affects the human body. The economies of certain countries may also begin to suffer from the deadly combination of heat and humidity. Krajick is the senior editor for science news at Columbia University's Earth Institute.

As you read, consider the following questions:

1. Why is humidity such a major factor in warming climates?
2. What is the relationship between humidity and the human body's ability to cool itself?
3. How might economies suffer because of high levels of heat and humidity?

C limate scientists say that killer heat waves will become increasingly prevalent in many regions as climate warms.

"Humidity May Prove Breaking Point for Some Areas as Temperatures Rise, Says Study," by Kevin Krajick, Earth Institute Columbia University, December 22, 2017. Reprinted by permission.

However, most projections leave out a major factor that could worsen things: humidity, which can greatly magnify the effects of heat alone. Now, a new global study projects that in coming decades the effects of high humidity in many areas will dramatically increase. At times, they may surpass humans' ability to work or, in some cases, even survive. Health and economies would suffer, especially in regions where people work outside and have little access to air conditioning. Potentially affected regions include large swaths of the already muggy southeastern United States, the Amazon, western and central Africa, southern areas of the Mideast and Arabian peninsula, northern India and eastern China.

"The conditions we're talking about basically never occur now—people in most places have never experienced them," said lead author Ethan Coffel, a graduate student at Columbia University's Lamont-Doherty Earth Observatory. "But they're projected to occur close to the end of the century." The study will appear this week in the journal Environmental Research Letters.

Warming climate is projected to make many now-dry areas dryer, in part by changing precipitation patterns. But by the same token, as global temperatures rise, the atmosphere can hold more water vapor. That means chronically humid areas located along coasts or otherwise hooked into humid-weather patterns may only get more so. And, as many people know, muggy heat is more oppressive than the "dry" kind. That is because humans and other mammals cool their bodies by sweating; sweat evaporates off the skin into the air, taking the excess heat with it. It works nicely in the desert. But when the air is already crowded with moisture— think muggiest days of summer in the city—evaporation off the skin slows down, and eventually becomes impossible. When this cooling process halts, one's core body temperature rises beyond the narrow tolerable range. Absent air conditioning, organs strain and then start to fail. The results are lethargy, sickness and, in the worst conditions, death.

Using global climate models, the researchers in the new study mapped current and projected future "wet bulb" temperatures, which reflect the combined effects of heat and humidity. (The measurement is made by draping a water-saturated cloth over the bulb of a conventional thermometer; it does not correspond directly to air temperature alone.) The study found that by the 2070s, high wet-bulb readings that now occur maybe only once a year could prevail 100 to 250 days of the year in some parts of the tropics. In the southeast United States, wet-bulb temperatures now sometimes reach an already oppressive 29 or 30 degrees Celsius; by the 2070s or 2080s, such weather could occur 25 to 40 days each year, say the researchers.

Lab experiments have shown wet-bulb readings of 32 degrees Celsius are the threshold beyond which many people would have trouble carrying out normal activities outside. This level is rarely reached anywhere today. But the study projects that by the 2070s or 2080s the mark could be reached one or two days a year in the US southeast, and three to five days in parts of South America, Africa, India and China. Worldwide, hundreds of millions of people would suffer. The hardest-hit area in terms of human impact, the researchers say, will probably be densely populated northeastern India.

"Lots of people would crumble well before you reach wet-bulb temperatures of 32 C, or anything close," said coauthor Radley Horton, a climate scientist at Lamont-Doherty. "They'd run into terrible problems." Horton said the results could be "transformative" for all areas of human endeavor—"economy, agriculture, military, recreation."

The study projects that some parts of the southern Mideast and northern India may even sometimes hit 35 wet-bulb degrees Celsius by late century—equal to the human skin temperature, and the theoretical limit at which people will die within hours without artificial cooling. Using a related combined heat/humidity measure, the so-called heat index, this would be the equivalent of nearly 170 degrees Fahrenheit of "dry" heat. But the heat index, invented in the 1970s to measure the "real feel" of moist summer weather, actually ends at 136; anything above that is literally off the chart.

On the bright side, the paper says that if nations can substantially cut greenhouse-gas emissions in the next few decades, the worst effects could be avoided.

Only a few weather events like those projected have ever been recorded. Most recent was in Iran's Bandar Mahshahr, on July 31, 2015. The city of more than 100,000 sits along the Persian Gulf, where seawater can warm into the 90s Fahrenheit, and offshore winds blow moisture onto land. On that day, the "dry" air temperature alone was 115 degrees Fahrenheit; saturated with moisture, the air's wet bulb reading neared the 35 C fatal limit, translating to a heat index of 165 Fahrenheit.

Bandar Mahshahr's infrastructure is good and electricity cheap, so residents reported adapting by staying in air-conditioned buildings and vehicles, and showering after brief ventures outside. But this may not be an option in other vulnerable places, where many people don't have middle-class luxuries.

"It's not just about the heat, or the number of people. It's about how many people are poor, how many are old, who has to go outside to work, who has air conditioning," said study coauthor Alex de Sherbinin of Columbia's Center for International Earth Science Information Network. De Sherbinin said that even if the weather does not kill people outright or stop all activity, the necessity of working on farms or in other outdoor pursuits in such conditions can bring chronic kidney problems and other damaging health effects. "Obviously, the tropics will suffer the greatest," he said. Questions of how human infrastructure or natural ecosystems might be affected are almost completely unexplored, he said.

Only a handful of previous studies have looked at the humidity issue in relation to climate change. It was in 2010 that a paper in the Proceedings of the National Academy of Sciences proposed the 35-degree survivability limit. In 2015, researchers published a paper in the journal *Nature Climate Change* that mapped areas in the southern Mideast and Persian Gulf regions as vulnerable to extreme conditions. There was another this year in the journal *Science Advances*, zeroing in on the densely populated, low-lying

Ganges and Indus river basins. The new study builds on this earlier research, extending the projections globally using a variety of climate models and taking into account future population growth.

Elfatih Eltahir, a professor of hydrology and climate at the Massachusetts Institute of Technology who has studied the issue in the Mideast and Asia, said the new study "is an important paper which emphasizes the need to consider both temperature and humidity in defining heat stress."

Climate scientist Steven Sherwood of the University of New South Wales, who proposed the 35-degree survivability limit, said he was skeptical that this threshold could be reached as soon as the researchers say. Regardless, he said, "the basic point stands." Unless greenhouse emissions are cut, "we move toward a world where heat stress is a vastly greater problem than it has been in the rest of human history. The effects will fall hardest on hot and humid regions."

In the United States Climate Change Has Made Restoration Ecologists Change Course

Maya L. Kapoor

Climate change is definitely beginning to affect Earth in terms of human habitation and agriculture. But in the following viewpoint Maya L. Kapoor shows that it also affects the restoration of certain environments, such as deserts in the southwestern United States. Environmental restoration projects must now consider the functions of ecosystems, as well as the future of these places and not just focus on what they were like in the past. Kapoor is an associate editor at High Country News.

As you read, consider the following questions:

1. How is climate change affecting environmental restoration in the southwest?
2. Why is it important for environmental restoration efforts to think about the future as well as the past?
3. Why are some restoration practitioners now focusing on ecosystem functions?

Carianne Campbell remembers the exact moment she fell in love with the Sonoran Desert. As a botany major in college, she joined a class field trip to Organ Pipe Cactus National

"Climate change is making it harder to revive damaged land," by Maya L. Kapoor, High Country News, June 29, 2018. Reprinted by permission.

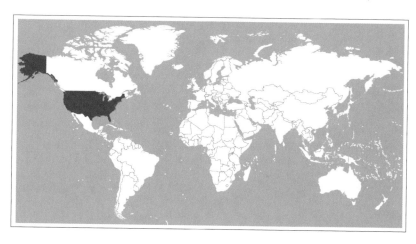

Monument on the southern border of Arizona, arriving and setting up camp in the dark. Emerging from her tent the next morning, Campbell, who grew up on the East Coast, caught her first glimpse of enormous saguaros, clustered organ pipes and bright desert wildflowers. She knew immediately that she wanted to work in this kind of landscape.

Today, Campbell is the restoration director for Sky Island Alliance, a nonprofit conservation organization based in Tucson, Arizona. She leads efforts to re-establish native plant communities in "sky islands"—isolated, ecologically rich mountain ranges that dot southeastern Arizona and New Mexico and northern Sonora, Mexico, and serve as home to some 7,000 species of plants and animals. Under Campbell's guidance, Sky Island Alliance restores riparian habitat that's been overrun by invasive species, such as fountaingrass, which crowds out local species and transforms the desert into fire-prone grassland.

The point of Campbell's job used to be relatively straightforward: She attempted to conserve local biodiversity by re-establishing the wild spaces where native plant and animal species once lived. But given the planet's rapid climate shifts, the connections between wild organisms and their ecosystems are fraying, forcing restoration biologists, including Campbell, to rethink the purpose of their work. It no longer helps to remember what a site looked like

20 years ago. "We need to be thinking about what it's going to be like 20 years into the future," she said.

In the early 1980s, ecological restoration was much like cleaning up after a rowdy house party: trying to return a degraded habitat to its former pristine condition. Project managers focused on returning the right numbers and species of plants—and by extension, animals—to places that had been logged, mined, invaded by nonnative species or otherwise altered by people. "I've always been taught that restoration is about taking a degraded site and restoring it back to what it was before the disturbance," Campbell said.

But increasingly, scientists who study ecosystems, as well as land managers who do restoration work, are questioning that model of ecological restoration, which relies on the idea of a stable "climax community," even though many ecosystems are always changing.

The West's forests, for one, are much more dynamic than many people realize. Notwithstanding individual tree outliers, such as millennia-old redwoods and bristlecone pines, most North American forest ecosystems are, at most, 400 or 500 years old, according to Don Falk, a forest ecologist at the University of Arizona. Reasons vary, from a severe drought in the late 1500s, to 1800s tree harvesting by Euro-Americans. Today, forests continue to undergo constant change. "Many of the forests we look at are in post-fire recovery, we just don't see it," Falk said. Outbreaks of insects such as bark beetles, which can decimate forests, add to the constant change. "We want to think of the primeval old-growth forest as having this stable characteristic, until we come along and introduce disturbance ... but the idea of forests in equilibrium is probably wrong." Indeed, events ranging from volcanic eruptions to the Pleistocene ice age have left their mark on the West's forests.

But with climate change, landscape-level transformations are happening faster and becoming more extreme. As the West becomes warmer and drier, the idea of "recovery" becomes increasingly unrealistic. Instead, ecosystems transform, such as in northern New Mexico, where Gambel oaks may replace pine forest after

Europe Faces Droughts, Floods, and Storms as Climate Change Speeds Up

Europe's Atlantic-facing countries will suffer heavier rainfalls, greater flood risk, more severe storm damage and an increase in "multiple climatic hazards," according to the most comprehensive study of Europe's vulnerability to climate change yet. Temperatures in mountain ranges such as the Alps and the Pyrenees are predicted to soar to glacier-melting levels, while the Mediterranean faces a "drastic" increase in heat extremes, droughts, crop failure and forest fires. Europe and the entire northern hemisphere are warming at a quicker pace than elsewhere, to the extent that tropical diseases such as West Nile fever are expected to spread across northern France by mid-century.

Earlier this month, Nasa, Noaa and the Met Office confirmed that 2016 had broken the record for the hottest year ever previously held by 2015, which had itself broken the record that had been held by 2014. The new EEA report finds that land temperatures in Europe in the last decade were 1.5C warmer than the pre-industrial age, although near-surface temperatures—measured at a metre above ground level—were only 0.83C-0.89C warmer. Over the course of this century, the study expects average global sea levels to rise between 1.5-2 metres, potentially threatening low-lying areas including south Florida, Bangladesh and Shanghai.

Frogs, birds, butterflies and insects are already advancing their life cycles as springs arrive earlier, but local extinctions of some species are being reported. "Species are adapting but not as fast as the climate is changing and this may cause disturbances in the equilibrium of ecosystems," Bruyninckx said. Butterflies and birds were already migrating northwards to the poles, he added.

This trend is only likely to deepen as heat extremes in central Europe grow stronger, while the boreal forests of Scandinavia experience less snow, river ice, and an increasing risk of winter storms and pest infestations. On the positive side, the region's hydropower and summer tourism potential are likely to increase, even as a reverse trend occurs in the Mediterranean.

Europe's thermal growing season is now 10 days longer than in 1992, with delays to the end of the season more dramatic than the advance of its start. In countries such as Spain, warmer conditions are expected to shift crop cultivation to the winter.

"Europe faces droughts, floods and storms as climate change accelerates," by Arthur Neslen, Guardian News and Media Limited, January 25, 2017.

a fire. "This is really a vexing problem for the field of restoration ecology, because our first instinct—and it's not wrong—is always to want to put it back to the way it was before we screwed things up," Falk said.

Restoration ecologists, in other words, no longer know how to define success. "The dilemma for the field of restoration is, it's almost damned if you do, damned if you don't," Falk said. "If you try to go back to 1850, it's just going to be a nonstarter, because the climate has moved on, and lots of other things have moved on. But if you're not restoring to a reference condition, then are you just sort of playing God and inventing new landscapes?"

This identity crisis is global: This year, at conferences from Iceland to Washington state, the Society for Ecological Restoration is grappling with the question of restoration during climate change.

Instead of trying to re-establish a checklist of plants and animals, as they might have in the past, some restoration practitioners are now focusing on ecosystem functions. For Campbell, that means worrying about pollinators, including birds, bats and insects, in the sky islands. Across the West, spring is thawing earlier and broiling into summer faster, and the region is getting hotter and drier overall, creating a mismatch between periods when pollinators need flowers and the times and places where those flowers are available. "How can I use various plant species in ways to ease that?" Campbell said.

Campbell keeps climate change and pollinators in mind when she's selecting native vegetation to plant. A low-elevation site might have red, tubular flowers in the spring, for example, and then again in September, but none during the hottest summer months. "I could plug in a species like desert honeysuckle, which would be blooming in that interim time, and providing a more constant source of nectar," she said.

Research on the timing of flowers and pollinator arrivals supports Campbell's concerns, although scientists don't yet know the consequences of these mismatches. Nicole Rafferty, a University of California, Riverside ecologist, studied the flowering schedule of manzanita, a mountain shrub with wine-red stems and glossy leaves, in the sky islands. The timing of the winter rains determines the appearance of manzanita blossoms, which are among the first mountain flowers each spring. But with winter rains arriving later, manzanitas are not flowering in time to feed the earliest native bees. Those later-flowering manzanitas also end up growing less fruit, which mule deer, black bears and other animals eat. Most plants have a wide enough variety of pollinators so that they won't disappear entirely, Rafferty said, but the fate of those pollinators is harder to predict.

Overall, Campbell's goal is still to conserve as much biodiversity as possible in the sky islands, where each mountain range has its own unique combination of plants and animals. But she knows she can't simply reassemble historic plant communities. "Certainly now, we (take) a forward view," Campbell said. "How is this (species) going to be durable into an uncertain future, where there's going to be larger, more intense wildfires, and more erosion, flooding, drought, all of those things?"

She's had to adapt how she uses native species, because of the changing rainfall patterns. For many years, Sky Island Alliance planted native vegetation in the spring, following the winter rains. But two years ago, Campbell noticed that most of the plants died. With spring arriving earlier and becoming hotter, "there's not enough time for those new plants to become established, and then be able to go dormant to make it through to monsoon season, and become good members of their vegetation society," Campbell said. She has stopped spring planting altogether at restoration sites, waiting instead until after the summer monsoon rains.

The new focus of ecological restoration is "less about identifying the particular species, and more about the traits," Elise Gornish, a cooperative extension specialist at the University of Arizona, said. Gornish surveyed almost 200 California managers, including master gardeners, ranchers, nonprofits, federal employees and others, about nonnative species. Close to half of her respondents, including most of the federal employees she interviewed, already used nonnative plants in restoration projects, often for erosion control. One reason was that they were less expensive. But almost 40 percent of the managers also contemplated using nonnatives because of climate change.

"It's clear that folks are really, really concerned about climate change and restoration," she said. "A lot of folks wouldn't use the term 'climate change' to describe their challenges; they would say things like 'drought,' 'changing environmental conditions.' " But the bottom line is the same: "Practices people have been using historically, and probably pretty successfully, and things that are now policies among the federal agencies … are not successful anymore," she said.

Some plant populations, for example, are responding to climate change by moving up in elevation and in latitude. "What this suggests is that if you're in your site that needs restoration, the plants from that area are probably no longer well-adapted to the new conditions of that area," Gornish said. This raises prickly questions about whether or not to start using plants from farther south and lower elevations, or even from entirely different regions. "People get extremely nervous, and with good reason, when you start talking about moving plants around," Gornish said. The US has not had a good track record with introduced species. "Some of our most noxious invasives, like tamarisk or buffelgrass, are things we planted 80 years ago," she said.

Not that long ago, the inclusion of nonnative plants species in restoration projects "was heretical," Falk agreed. Now, however, those species may be the best-adapted flora for a region's changing climate. But for Falk, managing for functions more than for species is still ecological restoration. It's always been true that, ultimately, "you're trying to maintain the ability of a system to adapt," he said.

For her part, Campbell is learning to reconsider the role of exotic species on the landscape. For example, she sometimes spares bird-of-paradise, an evergreen shrub in the pea family that is native to Uruguay and Argentina, in her restoration planning. A fast-growing ornamental with feathery leaves and bright red and orange flowers, bird-of-paradise thrives in the Southwest's disturbed landscapes, where it can crowd out native species. But removing the plant now may actually rob hummingbirds and other pollinators of meals. "It flowers opportunistically with rain," Campbell said, "so in summer months, it can be the only flowers available."

Periodical and Internet Sources Bibliography

The following articles have been selected to supplement the diverse views presented in this chapter.

Australian Academy of Science, "How do we expect climate to evolve in the future?" Australian Academy of Science, 2018. https://www.science.org.au/learning/general-audience/science-booklets-0/science-climate-change/4-how-do-we-expect-climate

Dēmos, "The Price Tag Of Being Young: Climate Change And Millennials' Economic Future." Dēmos, August 22, 2016. https://www.demos.org/publication/price-tag-being-young-climate-change-and-millennials-economic-future

Environmental Protection Agency, "Climate Change Science: Future of Climate Change." Environmental Protection Agency, January 2017. https://19january2017snapshot.epa.gov/climate-change-science/future-climate-change_.html

Exploritorium, "Looking Ahead." Exploratorium Global Climate Change Explorer, 2018. https://www.exploratorium.edu/climate/looking-ahead

Jon Mooallem, "Our Climate Future Is Actually Our Climate Present." *New York Times Magazine*, April 19, 2017. https://www.nytimes.com/2017/04/19/magazine/our-climate-future-is-actually-our-climate-present.html

NASA, "How Climate is Changing." NASA Global Climate Change: Vital Signs of the Planet. https://climate.nasa.gov/effects/

National Center for Atmospheric Research, "Predictions of Future Global Climate." National Center for Atmospheric Research, 2018. https://scied.ucar.edu/longcontent/predictions-future-global-climate

NOAA, "Future Climate." NOAA Climate.gov. https://www.climate.gov/maps-data/primer/future-climate

Dr. Petra Tschakert, "Future Climate Changes, Risks and Impacts." IPCC, 2013. http://www.climatechange2013.org/images/uploads/tschakert14SYRbern.pdf

US Global Change Research Program, "Future Climate Change."
https://nca2014.globalchange.gov/report/our-changing-climate/
future-climate-change

David Wallace-Wells, "The Uninhabitable Earth." *New York
Magazine*, July 10, 2017. http://nymag.com/intelligencer/2017/07/
climate-change-earth-too-hot-for-humans.html

For Further Discussion

Chapter 1

1. Why do you think that some politicians claim that climate change is not real?
2. What proof do scientists use to demonstrate that climate change is real?

Chapter 2

1. Should climate migration be treated the same as migration for political or disaster reasons?
2. How do you think countries should cope with the possibility of a large number of climate migrants seeking refuge?

Chapter 3

1. Why do you think climate change and population migration are political issues?
2. Do you think that the global community should, and can, develop common goals and policies concerning climate change?

Chapter 4

1. Do you think climate change can be reversed? Why or why not?
2. What do you believe is the most serious issue surrounding climate change and the future?

Organizations to Contact

The editors have compiled the following list of organizations concerned with the issues debated in this book. The descriptions are derived from materials provided by the organizations. All have publications or information available for interested readers. The list was compiled on the date of publication of the present volume; the information provided here may change. Be aware that many organizations take several weeks or longer to respond to inquiries, so allow as much time as possible.

Center for Climate and Energy Solutions (C2ES)
2101 Wilson Boulevard
Suite 550
Arlington, VA 22201
phone: (703) 516-4146
email: info@C2ES.org
website: www.c2es.org

C2ES is an independent, nonpartisan, nonprofit organization working to create practical solutions to climate change. It supports policies and actions to reduce greenhouse gas emissions, promote clean energy, and strengthen resilience to climate impacts. One of its major objectives is to create a national market-based program to reduce emissions cost-effectively.

Citizens' Climate Lobby
1330 Orange Avenue #309
Coronado, CA 92118
phone: (619) 437-7142
email: via website
website: www.citizensclimatelobby.org

The Citizens' Climate Lobby is a nonprofit, nonpartisan, grassroots advocacy organization focused on national policies to address climate change. It trains and supports volunteers to build relationships with elected officials, the media, and their local community to work toward the adoption of fair, effective, and sustainable climate change solutions.

Climate Action Network International (CAN)
International Address
Khaldeh, Dakdouk building, 3rd floor
Mount Lebanon—Lebanon
phone: +961.1.447192
email: administration@climatenetwork.org
website: www.climatenetwork.org

CAN is a worldwide network of over 1,300 nongovernmental organizations in over 120 countries. These groups work to promote government and individual action to limit human-induced climate change to ecologically sustainable levels. They share information and work to develop strategies for addressing international, regional, and national climate issues.

The Climate Reality Project
750 9th Street NW
Suite 520
Washington, DC 20001
phone: (202) 628-1999
email: via website
website: www.climaterealityproject.org

The mission of the Climate Reality Project is to catalyze a global solution to the climate crisis by making urgent action a necessity across every level of society. Urgent actions include cutting greenhouse gas emissions, speeding the global shift to renewable energy, reducing the use of fossil fuels, and urging world leaders to strengthen and honor their Paris Agreement commitments concerning carbon emissions.

Environmental Protection Agency (EPA)
1200 Pennsylvania Avenue, N.W.
Washington, DC 20460
phone: (202) 564-4700
email: via website
website: www.epa.gov

The EPA's mission is to protect human health and the environment. As part of this mission, it is creating adaptation plans for dealing with climate change and its effects on humans and the environment. It also provides information on green energy and reducing the causes of climate change.

Intergovernmental Panel on Climate Change (IPCC)
c/o World Meteorological Organization
7 bis Avenue de la Paix C.P. 2300
CH- 1211 Geneva 2, Switzerland
phone : +41-22-730-8208/54/84
email: IPCC-Sec@wmo.int
website: www.wmo.int

The IPCC is the leading international group for the assessment of climate change. It was established in 1988 to provide the world with a clear scientific view on the current state of knowledge in climate change and its potential impacts.

National Oceanic and Atmospheric Administration (NOAA)
1401 Constitution Avenue NW, Room 5128
Washington, DC 20230
phone: (828) 271-4800
email: via website
website: www.noaa.gov

NOAA is a federal agency that works to keep members of the public informed of the changing environment around them. Its services include daily weather forecasts, severe storm warnings, climate monitoring, fisheries management, coastal restoration, and support for marine commerce. It also provides information about climate change, its causes, and its effects on people and environments.

Natural Resources Defense Council (NRDC)
40 West 20th Street
11th floor
New York, NY 10011
phone: (212) 727-2700
email: nrdcinfo@nrdc.org
website: www.nrdc.org

The NRDC's mission is to safeguard Earth, its people, its plants and animals, and the natural systems on which all life depends. It partners with businesses, political leaders, scientists, lawyers, and policy advocates across the globe to combat pollution and other threats to the planet. Its newest campaign is to prevent catastrophic climate change by transforming the way people produce electricity, make the things they need, and move people and goods around.

Union of Concerned Scientists
2 Brattle Square
Cambridge, MA 02138-3780
phone: (800) 666-8276
email: via website
website: www.ucsusa.org

The Union of Concerned Scientists, a nonprofit organization, was founded to help scientists and engineers develop and implement innovative, practical solutions to some of the planet's biggest problems, including climate change and the need to find sustainable ways to create food, energy, and transportation.

Yale Program on Climate Change Communication (YPCCC)
Yale School of Forestry & Environmental Studies
195 Prospect Street (Kroon Hall)
New Haven, CT 06511
phone: (203) 432-5055
email: climatechange@yale.edu
website: www.climatecommunication.yale.edu/

YPCCC, part of Yale University, conducts scientific research on public climate change knowledge, attitudes, policy preferences, and behavior, and the underlying psychological, cultural, and political factors that influence them. It also engages the public in climate change science and solutions, in partnership with governments, media organizations, companies, and civil society, and with a daily, national radio program, Yale Climate Connections.

Bibliography of Books

Paul Collier and Alexander Betts, *Refuge: Rethinking Refugee Policy in a Changing World*. New York, NY: Oxford University Press, 2017.

Riley E. Dunlap and Robert J. Brulle, eds., *Climate Change and Society: Sociological Perspectives*. New York, NY: Oxford University Press, 2015.

Charles Eisenstein, *Climate—A New Story*. Berkeley, CA: North Atlantic Books, 2018.

Jeff Goodell, *The Water Will Come: Rising Seas, Sinking Cities, and the Remaking of the Civilized World*. Boston, MA: Back Bay Books, 2018.

Rebecca E. Hirsch, *Climate Migrants: On the Move in a Warming World*. New York, NY: Twenty-First Century Books, 2016.

Avidan Kent, *Climate Refugees (Routledge Studies in Environmental Migration, Displacement and Resettlement)*. New York, NY: Routledge, 2018.

Elizabeth Kolbert, *Field Notes from a Catastrophe: Man, Nature, and Climate Change*. New York, NY: Bloomsbury, 2015.

Elizabeth Kolbert, *The Sixth Extinction: An Unnatural History*. New York, NY: Picador, 2015.

Michael E. Mann and Lee R. Kump, *Dire Predictions: The Visual Guide to the Findings of the IPCC, 2nd Edition*. New York, NY: DK Publishing, 2015.

Robert A. Mcleman, *Climate and Human Migration: Past Experiences, Future Challenges*. New York, NY: Cambridge University Press, 2013.

New York Times Educational Publishing, *Climate Refugees: How Global Change Is Displacing Millions (In the Headlines)*.

New York, NY: New York Times Educational Publishing, 2018.

Joseph Romm, *Climate Change: What Everyone Needs to Know*, 2nd ed. New York, NY: Oxford University Press, 2018.

John R. Wennersten and Denise Robbins, *Rising Tides: Climate Refugees in the Twenty-First Century*. Bloomington, IN: Indiana University Press, 2017.

Index

W